"Laughter is the only exerci[...]ity of it from this new book by Jeff Allen and Martha Bolton! Each of them is a wonderful comic talent who has been making me laugh for years. If you're ready for a laughter workout, you're gonna love this book!"

Mark Lowry, comedian and singer/songwriter

"There is no doubt that marriage and family life is a serious topic in today's church. We men must be reminded often that while there are always problems and concerns living with our wives and kids, there is also much that brings us joy and laughter. In *My Life as a Bystander*, Jeff and Martha have crafted a wonderful reminder for us all that our home life is or should be the best facet of life. While giving us plenty to laugh about, they have also laced the humor with biblical reinforcement for building a home to the glory of God."

Tommy Nelson, pastor, Denton Bible Church, Denton, Texas, popular author of *The Book of Romance* and *The Problem of Life with God*

"There are the obvious places where I believe God speaks to me: through the Word, through my pastor, or through my family. But it's always so refreshing when—from some unexpected place—I get inspired, nurtured, or refreshed. That's what happens to me when I hear Jeff Allen's comedy. I'm entertained, I'm amused, and in the end I'm refreshed and challenged. Jeff has a way of making me think, ponder, and reflect because his comedy is inspired. The road Jeff takes you down—getting to his point—is absolutely hilarious. And the destination is always profound. Jeff has a true gift—not just to make you laugh but to make you understand and see God's redemptive grace. I'm so glad to see Jeff use his gifts for eternal purposes. Isn't it amazing to think there would be people in heaven because someone here made them laugh."

Michael W. Smith, singer/songwriter

My Life as a Bystander

For Better or Worse and
Everything in Between

My Life
as a
Bystander

Jeff Allen
and Martha Bolton

BROADMAN
&HOLMAN
PUBLISHERS

NASHVILLE, TENNESSEE

© 2005 by Jeff Allen

All rights reserved

Printed in the United States of America

13-digit ISBN: 978-0-8054-3166-7

10-digit ISBN: 0-8054-3166-7

Published by Broadman & Holman Publishers,
Nashville, Tennessee

Dewey Decimal Classification: 306.8
Subject Headings: MARRIAGE—HUMOR
                   FAMILY—HUMOR \ MEN—HUMOR

Unless noted otherwise, Scripture verses are from the Holman
Christian Standard Bible, © 1999, 2000, 2002, 2003 by Holman
Bible Publishers, Nashville, Tennessee; all rights reserved.
Other versions quoted are NIV, the Holy Bible, New
International Version, © 1973, 1978, 1984 by International
Bible Society; and NKJV, the New King James Version, ©
1979, 1980, 1982, Thomas Nelson, Inc., Publishers.

1 2 3 4 5 6 7 8 9 10 09 08 07 06 05

I dedicate this book to
those in my life who have made the greatest sacrifices:
The love of my life, my wife, Tami, who has
put up with more than any wife should have had to.
My boys, Aaron and Ryan, until you have
children of your own, you will never understand
how much I really love you; thank you.
My mom and dad, thank you for loving me
more than I ever knew.

—*Jeff Allen*

To my husband, Russ, for the love, support,
and all the ink he's had to buy over the years.
And to my ever-growing circle of friends and family
who make life the joy that it is.

—*Martha Bolton*

Contents

Foreword

Jeff Allen is a funny man. He is also drop-dead serious on occasion. And despite his protestations to the contrary, he is way more than a bystander. His wit and observations about life, love, kids, and marriage have not only gotten him "involved" in the lives of the artistic community with whom we both travel, but they have drawn his audience into a self-examination more effectively than any psychiatrist I know. Not only does his humor dig around in our corporate and personal hidden psyches; it precipitates soul introspection as well. Trust me. Go hear Jeff, and you'll find yourself laughing all the way to the altar.

In this book Jeff delves into the inner sanctum of family life, exposing such carefully guarded workings as a mom's skill at "selective listening" while dad's mind "drifts off to golf courses unknown," a teen-ager's logic (who needs showers or clean underwear when there's a perfectly good lake to swim in every day?), and city children's secrets for defending themselves and their booty in rough neighborhoods on Halloween night (lobbing popcorn balls at a bully's head, splitting it like a cantaloupe). He gives advice on how to tell "woman's work" from "man's work" in a perfect marriage and gives tips for everyday living, such as don't gargle shampoo or tap dance on glass-top coffee tables.

He also raises theological questions: Why didn't God make babies so that they would sprout their teeth in one crop and parents would know when it was time to start solid foods, and does God have hair on the back of His neck that stands up when *we* ask *Him* certain questions?

On a more practical level, Jeff, from all his experience on the road, gives creative travel tips, like using navel lint as a wet-wipe for freshening up on long Greyhound bus trips and not using eight-dollar disposable cameras to photograph the Grand Canyon from the airplane window at thirty thousand feet.

Yes, this collection of observations is far more invasive than its humble title suggests. When you're finished, you will be certain that even bystanders end up very much involved.

—*Gloria Gaither*
Author/Lyricist

Acknowledgments

My manager and good friend Lenny Sisselman, who next to my wife knows me better than anyone and despite that knowledge still believes in me—thank you for that belief.

My good friend Chaz Corzine, everything in this business begins with a door opening. Thank you for selflessly opening doors. I will never be able to repay you.

Martha Bolton, my coauthor, who took all the incoherent drivel I sent her and sent it back not only coherent but with all the commas and periods in the right places. Thank you—I'd still be on paragraph 1 if not for you.

I would also be remiss if I did not thank all the strangers in those twelve step rooms across the country, who for years showed me God's grace by allowing me to be part of their "club." Despite my "cheerful" personality, thank you for allowing me to "keep coming back." It does work if you work it.

Jeff Patterson, thank you for your passion; it is contagious.

The whole gang at Nashville Speakers—thank you.

Last but not least, my good friend Phil Glasgow and his wife Carol, who took seriously Jesus' command to make disciples of all men. They are an example of people who not only read God's Word but actually live it. Hopefully, when I grow up I will be like you. Thank you not only from me but from

Tami, Aaron, and Ryan for your dinnertime prayers. I didn't deserve it.

No one does life alone. I hope you all understand how much I appreciate all you do for me.

—Jeff

CHAPTER ONE

My Life
as a Bystander

Greetings, bystanders. You must be a bystander or you wouldn't be holding this book in the first place. And now that it's in your hands, you know you have to take it home and read it. Why? Because it offers the solace of a fellow bystander. Bystanders need the company of other bystanders. We need to be with those who have spent their entire lives just trying to stay out of everyone's way, not rocking the boat and basically just minding their own business.

But the world won't let us mind our own business, will it? We want to watch life from the sidelines, but someone keeps throwing us the ball and telling us to run with it. We don't want to run with the ball . . . at least not in the direction they're pointing—which is right in the path of all those three-hundred-pound linebackers. We want to run toward the parking lot—away from danger, not into it. We want to lead the football team in a chorus of "Kumbaya." We don't enjoy confrontation. We'd much rather just stand there and cheer others on as they tackle their own linebackers in life. We'd rather ponder life than actually participate in it because that's what we bystanders do. We blend in. We adapt. We step aside. We nap. And we do it all while minding our own business.

I've been a bystander for as long as I can remember. It's my calling. I'm well experienced in the field of minding my own business. I don't like to be bothered, and I try not to bother other people. In fact, the very first thing I did when I came into this world was look around the birthing room and say, "Did I come at a bad time?"

If you ask me, involvement is overrated. Apathy can sometimes be a good thing. At least it's never really hurt anyone. Take Noah's neighbors, for example. They were bystanders. They sat around watching him work on that ark day in and day out without so much as offering to hold a nail for him. They just stood there and watched, and it didn't hurt their . . . OK, bad example.

But what about Benjamin Franklin's neighbors? They must have watched him from their windows as he flew his kite in the middle of that thunderstorm. And like true bystanders, they didn't get in his way. They had no idea what he was working on, of course. All they knew was that at the moment the electric jolt went through his kite and snaked its way to the key he was holding, their television sets went on.

The world needs bystanders. Without those of us who do nothing, how would anyone ever be able to tell who's doing anything? Amazing achievements would look ordinary because we'd have nothing to compare them with. Nobel Prizes would be mailed to more houses than Publishers

Clearing House notices. Einstein, Edison, Churchill, and all the other overachievers owe their many accolades to the bystanders of their day.

But don't fall for the misconception that being a bystander is synonymous with being lazy or frivolous. Though close in meaning, there are subtle differences among the terms. Bystanders don't dispute the importance of work; they just prefer to stay on the fringes of it or let someone else do it. They know their apathy can ultimately be for the overall good of the project. For instance, I was once part of a Habitat for Humanity project, and after about half an hour of messing up various parts of the project (apparently, closets have no need for a fireplace), I discovered that my true calling was elsewhere.

I left the construction unit of the project and joined the morale-boosting team. I walked the grounds, picking up trash and making jokes about what a useless slug I was. I willingly sacrificed my dignity for the greater good of the project. People laughed, a few even nodded in agreement of my self-deprecating statements, and the day went a little quicker for everyone because of my efforts. In other words, I filled a need. But it's a need that fewer and fewer people are willing to fill today.

I'm a comedian by trade, and most of us comedians will readily admit to our bystander ways. We stand on the sidelines and observe truth. Then just for fun, we season our observations with the absurd. That's where the comedy is. We don't get too involved in changing the world because if the world were a perfect place, we'd be out of material. We are far more comfortable just watching others live life and commenting about it. But that's OK. We believe bystanders have a purpose, and we're fulfilling it.

Martha (my coauthor and prolific comedy writer) and I have written my life's adventures in hopes of readers laughing along with us and learning a life lesson or two—lessons that I have, of course, had to learn the hard way (bystanders can also be pretty stubborn).

But if you're still not convinced that this is a book you simply must have in your library, then let me present my case another way: I have two sons who are eating us out of house and home. I need the royalties. I also have to pay back a pretty hefty advance. And I enjoy golfing (if you are married to, dating, or have parented a golfer, you know how expensive this hobby can be). I like to eat too. Earlier in my career, I didn't get to do a lot of that, so I've been enjoying this new activity. I also have a beautiful wife who likes to shop and doesn't appreciate the clerk asking, "Do you have another credit card you can use, Mrs. Allen?"

Another reason for you to buy this book is to bump it onto the *New York Times* best-sellers list. Bill O'Reilly and Al Franken have spent enough time on the best-seller rack at Barnes and Noble. They need to let some of the little people have a chance now. I can't keep going down there every day and shifting my books to that rack. I'm starting to get stares from the employees.

You could also buy this book because of all the work that Martha and I put into it. At the beginning of this project, we had very little stress and certainly no panic. We had no words written yet either. The stress began after I spent the first advance check and continued until I spent the second advance check. When we approached the final deadline, the panic set in. Our computers began shooting chapters back and forth faster than you can say, "You've got mail." We've spent countless hours creating, writing, and fine-tuning this work, and as supportive as our spouses have been, we'd like to be able to make enough off this book to take them out to dinner.

But if you still need more convincing, then I appeal to you to purchase it because I sincerely believe you'll enjoy it. As things calm down and we begin to see the light at the end of the printer, I finally have time to sit back and reflect on what we've written. And out of my frustrations, humiliations, and failings, I hope you'll glean the salient truths of marriage, parenting, and life . . . and have a few laughs along the way.

"[He] said to them, 'Why have you been standing here all day doing nothing?'"
Matthew 20:6

CHAPTER TWO

I Don't Think So, Rash Boy!

The reason we are allowed to supervise our children for eighteen years (before sending them off to whatever they decide to do with the rest of their lives) is that it takes that long for them to get the basic habits of life down. Like hygiene. My son Ryan is fourteen years old and still requires constant reminders to brush his teeth. He has done everything possible to avoid this socially required ritual ever since his teeth tore through his gums in his first year or two of life.

And speaking of teething, don't you wonder why the Creator didn't come up with a less painful way for a baby to sprout teeth? Couldn't a full set of choppers just appear one morning while the kids are sitting in their high chair waiting for their oatmeal to cool? We'd see the mouthful of pearly whites and know that it's time for our little darling to start eating solid food. That certainly would beat all the countless nights of screaming, crying, and whining . . . and that's just from us parents.

I remember when Ryan was teething. We lived in an apartment complex with paper-thin walls. Ryan's teething pains were registering a 6.2 on the Richter scale. Apparently, a child's screaming is contagious because it didn't take long for our neighbors to begin screaming at us. One man even pounded on our wall one night and yelled, "TELL THAT KID TO SHUT UP!" And he was a monk who had taken a vow of silence.

I have to admit, we had never thought of just telling Ryan to shut up. Here we were walking him, rocking him, holding him close, and doing our best to comfort him. It hadn't occurred to us to just yell at him and tell him to shut up. Interesting concept, though. So I tried it. I did what our budding Dr.-Spock-of-a-neighbor had suggested. I screamed at the lad, "Shuuuuuuu-uuuuuuuuuuuuuuuuuuuuuuuutUuuuuuuuuuuuuuuP!" Amazingly enough, silence did follow. Just enough time for the lad to reload his lungs for the big one that followed. A scream came out of that youngster that blew the windows out of a passing 747.

Sometimes, parents really are better off following their own instincts.

All I have to say is, it's good that the decision of whether your children should have teeth is made by God and not left up to us parents. Because after the second or third tooth, many of us would be tempted to start evaluating how many teeth the child really needs to get by in life. I can honestly say it wouldn't take but about four nights of lost sleep for me to mumble to my wife, "Perhaps the child could live on soup his whole life."

Eventually the teeth did arrive, but only one at a time — not the thirty-two overnight that I was hoping for. But with teeth come responsibility, so right away his mother and I began to teach him the care and maintenance of enamel. We showed him how to squeeze the toothpaste out of the tube and to use a toothbrush without gagging himself to death.

Frankly, I don't understand why kids today have a problem with brushing their teeth. In this day and age of coddling our youth, corporations have come up with a whole slew of dental products just for kids, one of which is bubble-gum-flavored toothpaste. How cool is that? I had to brush my teeth with the peppermint-flavored caulk my father used to burn the acid deposits off our car battery. That's why he always insisted we put the cap back on the toothpaste tube. If any of that stuff ever fell on the sink, it would eat right through the Formica.

But what do my kids get to brush their teeth with? Bazooka bubble-gum-flavored toothpaste, that's what! What's next? Brownie mouthwash? If it sounds like I'm complaining, I am. My sons have no idea how good they have it. They've never had to gargle with the kind of mouthwash I had to endure. I won't divulge the product name, but you know which one I mean. It not only killed germs, but every living organism within a fifty-foot radius of your bathroom. My sons gargle with something akin to grape juice and whine about it. I just made one of them take a whiff of the mouthwash of my day and he passed out. Luckily, a second whiff brought him back around.

But as I said, we are fourteen years deep into this tooth-brushing ritual with Ryan, and it still hasn't hit home with him. His breath is wilting the houseplants, and he still thinks brushing teeth is an option.

He has the same attitude about his homework, making his bed, loading the dishwasher, and, of course, taking a shower. These are all things that he has been told to do his entire life, and yet he continues to need reminders to do them, unlike playing video games or watching television (those two activities seem to be instinctual). But personal hygiene? It seems that doesn't kick in until the dating years.

It truly boggles my mind how many nights we have had the following discussion.

"Hey, take a shower," I say.

"For what?" he says, with an incredulous look on his face.

"Do the letters *B* and *O* mean anything to you?" This is when I usually get the blank look, so I continue. "Come on, man, wash off some of those dead skin cells, will you? We all have to live here."

Reluctantly, he shuffles off to the shower like a prisoner going to work camp. I mean, this boy would rather get a spinal tap than take a shower. A friend of mine suggested just letting Ryan have it his way and allowing the fungus to grow on the boy until he learns his lesson. Or his clothes don't fit over the two inches of grime covering him. Yeah, he felt the young lad could scratch his way to learning about body rashes and athlete's foot. I have to admit, it sounded tempting, so I decided to heed his advice and not say anything more about his bathing.

You've heard the saying, "Let go and let God." Well, that's what I did. I figured if cleanliness was next to godliness, then maybe God could mix a little soap in with the next rainfall and make the boy presentable. Now, throwing up your hands in the face of a family dilemma is a typical bystander thing to do, but before soap clouds were predicted on the Weather Channel, the Boy Scouts saved me from myself.

Ryan enjoyed Scouting, and when he came home from a Scout meeting and announced that he wanted to go to camp this year, I was thrilled. He had been passing on this camp for years because of a bad camping experience he'd had when he was seven. He'd been stung by a bee, and his young brain deduced that camp was where bees hung out. There was no convincing him otherwise . . . until this year.

The camp was to be held in June, and if you don't know Southern summers, allow me to give you a brief description. Perhaps you've heard about Arizona's dry-heat theory. Well, in the South, it's wet heat; sauna comes to mind. During the summer, it can run about ninety and ninety — 90-degree heat and 90-percent humidity. Basically, my son was going to be living in a hamper for five days — a perfect opportunity for a fungus to grow among us, if you know what I mean.

Of course, as nice as it was that Ryan was finally going to give camp another try, we still encountered a few problems along the way, like packing. As most parents know, it's difficult to let go and let him (or her, if you happen to have daughters). You know your children need their independence, but in an odd sort of way, you want to be at their side to help them manage it.

My wife, Tami, in her naiveté, thought she would do Ryan a favor by packing his satchel for his week away from home. I say naiveté because she thought that he — like his bystander father — would jump at the opportunity to skip a menial chore.

I have been traveling for more than twenty-five years, and I have to tell you, if my wife ever offered to pack for me, I would not only jump at the chance but would also ask her if she was feeling all right since the head injury, knowing that surely a large object must have fallen on her noggin to elicit such an offer.

Ryan, however, didn't see his mom's offer as a gift. To him, it was an intrusion. So the two of them went about seven rounds, arguing over who would "get" to do the packing. My wife figured he needed help. My son wanted and needed independence and freedom of choice. I finally tag-teamed my son and offered backup. They say that's not always the best thing to do. But I asked my wife what the harm could be in letting the young Scout do it for himself. Then, just for kicks, I threw in, "You know, I am leaving tomorrow on a trip and could use a little help."

She threw a sock at me that could have easily put my eye out. So I decided the best thing for me to do was let them work it out alone.

At last, my wife acquiesced. My son thanked her for the offer, then retreated to his room to start packing for camp.

It may have been seven, no, I believe it was eight minutes later that Ryan came barreling out of his room, said that he was all done, and ran outside to play.

Done? How could it be? You can't pack for a five-day camp in only eight minutes! My wife and I decided to check out his handiwork. "Let's take a little field trip of our own," I said. We couldn't wait to see what a youth of his maturity and foresight would pack for such an expedition.

Going into his room when he wasn't there wasn't trespassing, we figured. After all, we pay the mortgage. And the utility bills. We even bought his overnight bag. So despite what the ACLU says, unzipping it and checking out his packing skills was our right as parents—our duty, even. Besides, this is the closest thing we get to exciting anymore. It was also the only way to satisfy our overwhelming curiosity as to exactly what an eight-minute packing job might look like.

We opened the overnight bag and, are you ready for this? Apparently, all our young man needed for five days on the road was two pairs of shorts, a couple pairs of socks, his Game Boy, and twenty-two games to go along with it. Getting away to commune with nature has changed a little since the emergence of more advanced technology.

Granted, we had expected to find some electronics. And at least two of the video games did have jungle themes. The shorts and socks were a nice touch too. But other than those few clothing items, our son hadn't packed one single thing that involved proper hygiene.

Needless to say, my wife and I unpacked his idea of suitable camp provisions and, instead, packed our idea of what he needed, removing the video games and the Game Boy in the process. We were counting on the fact that the lad wouldn't check his bag until he was hundreds of miles away at Camp Mildew.

The next morning, he woke up, dressed, and excitedly threw his bag into the van. We drove to the campgrounds and when we arrived, I so wanted to follow him to his cabin just to hear the ear-piercing wail that he would emit when he opened his bag and found a toothbrush, deodorant, and six pairs of clean under-wear in place of video games. I wanted to hear him telling his little buds, "Dude, I can't believe it. I got my dad's bag by mis-take!" Thinking about it makes me chuckle even today.

I should confess that Tami and I did place a small bet (just for fun, not cash) on how many pairs of underwear he would actually use. Tami went with three pairs. I wagered two.

As excited as Ryan was to go, we received a call on the fifth day of camp from Ryan's scoutmaster, who told us Ryan had to leave camp early because he was so full of "skeeter" bites and fungus. So Tami and I did the only thing we could do. We upped our wager, got in the car, and drove to the campground.

Now mind you, Ryan was in the woods of Tennessee for five days. Five days. In June. In Tennessee. And he had access to six clean pairs of underwear. Six pairs. But when we got to

Ryan's cabin (he happened to be out at the time) and checked his bag, we discovered that *all* of the underwear was still neatly folded. Let me repeat that. *All of the underwear was still neatly folded.* That means our son didn't even pull out a pair of clean ones, look at them, then throw them on the ground and say, "Naw, why bother?" He didn't even try to wad a few pairs into a ball and pretend that he had worn them. He didn't try to hide the fact that it hadn't once occurred to him to change his underwear in those five days!

Tami and I waited in our car while the scoutmaster drove the grounds to locate him. When he found Ryan, he dropped him off in front of the main building to walk the two hundred or so yards to our car.

As we watched our Sad Sack walking toward us, we could see that he was wearing the same clothes he'd been wearing when he left. His hair was literally plastered to his skull, his face was sunburned and swollen, and he was waddling as if straddling a fence. It was one of the most heartbreaking scenes of my life.

All right, who am I kidding? I burst out laughing. I was laughing so hard I couldn't catch my breath. But when he started to get in my car for the ride home, I caught my breath and held onto it (and my nose) for dear life.

"Whoa! Hold on there, Rash Boy. You're not getting in this car. Get the bungee cords out. We're strapping you to the roof like a deer and going through a car wash!"

Tami didn't let me strap him to the roof, though. She said it'd be too hazardous to drive with all the buzzards he'd attract. So we took him to the nearest hotel, rented a room for an hour, and let him take a long overdue shower. It was the first time we ever heard him say that it felt good to bathe.

Afterward, on our way home, I asked him if he had showered at all the entire week. He responded with a typical teenage answer, "For what? We swam all week."

Kids.

But it wasn't just Ryan who used that scholarly reasoning. He said that all the kids at the camp figured the swimming pool took care of their bathing needs. No soap, but plenty of chlorine. That fact alone should frighten every parent who sends the kids off to camp. Think about it: three or four hundred hygienically challenged boys all swimming in the same pool of water. There's not enough chlorine in the world to handle something like that. It's bacterial soup, a CDC nightmare.

When I expressed my disbelief that the Scouts would allow all these infested boys to swim together day after day, Ryan said, "We had *two* pools, Dad, not *one*."

To which I replied, "Which one did you swim in? The E coli wave pool or the salmonella slide 'n' splash?"

His mother and I have four more years to work on his hygiene before he's turned loose in the world as an adult. It's either that or buy a lot of air freshener.

"Martha, the dead man's sister, told Him, 'Lord, he already stinks. It's been four days.'"
John 11:39

CHAPTER THREE

Is There Paper in Heaven?

I once read that the ultimate sign of love and respect is listening to another human being. I love my children and respect them. They know they're in my comedy routine, and they love hearing the stories I tell about them. But years ago I made a mental note to really listen to them. (Mental notes are a bystander's version of a PDA. The problem is, though, you have to wait until senility to empty the hard drive.)

Like a lot of things in life, it's easier said than done. If you hung on every word your three-year-old said, your brain would literally explode by noon. In my case, that might not be too large of an explosion, but the point is, a nice balance needs to be achieved. It is important to listen to our kids, but if we allow them to blather on endlessly without ever being checked, they can keep us from getting our work done and putting food on the table. They can also begin to believe that the universe really does revolve around them. In other words, children need to learn manners.

I once read an article about parenting that said teaching children manners is abusive because it goes against their basic "nature." Can you believe that? What does this writer think the act of unleashing rude and obnoxious children on an unsuspecting world is? And merely teaching a child the words "excuse me" isn't a panacea either. On the surface it's polite, but sometimes kids feel the words "excuse me" give them the right to interrupt as often as they please. After about the 900th "excuse me," it might be time for parents to rethink that strategy.

Whenever my sons interrupt me with an "excuse me," I always give them the stock parental answer, "In a minute." This only works when they actually know how long a minute lasts. My son Aaron once had a twenty-minute conversation with me while I was on the telephone. I kept covering the receiver and asking him to give me a minute to finish my conversation.

"Excuse me, Dad," he said.

"In a minute, son. I'm on the phone."

"Is it a minute yet?"

"No."

"Is it now?"

"No."

"Now?"

"No."

This went on and on until it finally hit me. *The kid has no idea what a minute is!* Aren't epiphanies wonderful?

Ignoring a child's prattling isn't the answer either. Years ago, I was at a mall with my wife and our son Ryan. Trying to keep up with the latest parental technology, my wife had our son on a leash attached to her belt loop. That's right. My wife paid good money for one of those kid harnesses. Actually, I like the idea of a leash, and as I see it, there's nothing wrong with it if you are just walking through the mall. The kid just kind of flops around behind you like a long board behind a downed surfer. As long as we were in motion, everything was fine. The problems began when we stopped in the middle of the mall to briefly converse about which store to visit next.

As we were talking, our little one began to wrap himself around his mother's leg. Eventually, he ran out of leash, and like a dog that's wound himself around a tree, he couldn't figure out how to turn around and go back the other way. Now, literally pinned to his mother's thigh, the lad began to chant the chant. We all know what "the chant" is, don't we? We've heard it a thousand times in malls, grocery stores, and restaurants all over the globe. "Mommy, Mommy, Mommy, Mommy, Ma, Ma, Ma, Ma, Mom, Mom, Mom, Mom, Mommy, Mommy, Mommy, Mommy . . ."

I believe you get the point. The chant is relentless. The words never change, but like an old campfire song, the verses can go on forever. What my wife failed to recognize that day is that there is not a three-year-old alive who will say to himself, "Gee, Mom looks a little busy. Maybe I'll give it another minute and let her finish what she's doing, then we can properly focus on my request."

Three-year-olds don't process information like that. Sometimes husbands don't either, but that's a different chapter. So the chanting just kept going, and through all this, my wife continued to try to hold a conversation with me. But did she honestly think I could hear her over the chant? Apparently so because her lips were moving. Now, both of their voices just sort of blended together, so I heard, "Mommy, Mommy,

Mommy . . . food court . . . Mommy, Mommy . . . credit-card limit . . . Mommy, Mommy. Mommmmmmmmy."

I can't begin to tell you how frustrating this was for me. At one point, I started vibrating, and blood began to trickle out of my ears. Thankfully, at that moment some guy came to my aid and got on the public address system in the mall and announced, *"Please, lady, answer your child! Please answer your child!"*

There was even a mime in the mall that came over and slapped my wife with his padded white glove. Then he asked, "Is your name Mommy?" (I pause at this point to explain the severity of this mime's actions. You see, mimes are dedicated artists. It takes a tremendous amount of angst to get them to break character.)

Even though he's a fellow artist, I do feel that my painted little friend was way out of line when he mimed an attempt to maim my wife. So as a man, a father, and a husband, and I might add, totally against my bystander lifestyle, I went after that mime. It was the oddest thing too. I started to run, but it was as if I were running against a strong wind. I was stalled, but not completely. Then, just as I began to gain ground and was closing in on him, he somehow locked himself in a box (how do they do that?!). In the distance the chant began anew. As the vibrations resumed, I tried to climb into the box with him, hoping it was soundproof, but he wouldn't let me in. I thought mimes were by nature compassionate, caring human beings. Apparently I was wrong. One more myth destroyed.

Knowing what I had to do, I left the scene of the mime and returned to the scene of the chant. And this is where I come to the point of my story—the importance of listening to those you love.

As Tami continued to talk over the chant, I finally stopped her in midsentence. "I believe our son would like to talk to you," I said.

Tami looked a little annoyed at me, as if to say, "OK, let me show you something, Dad." She then stooped down and asked the little lad what it was he wanted to say. He put his chant on pause for a moment and said, "I forgot."

With that, Tami just smiled at me and winked triumphantly. She knew this answer long before he ever said it. Women know instinctively when a child needs to ask something important and when he is merely enjoying the melodious sound of his own voice. It's called "selective listening."

To raise children, all parents need certain tools. Patience, tolerance, love, and understanding are in the basic kit, but the bonus tool is selective listening, which comes as standard equipment in a woman's toolbox. I had to earn my selective listening tool—and every tool in my box, for that matter—the hard way.

Back when Ryan was three, I was working in my garage, minding my own business, pretending to be building something. I do this so I won't have to go in the house and do the chores my wife wants me to do. In other words, I was enjoying the day in true bystander form.

Ryan, who happened to be sitting at my feet just chatting away about everything and nothing, not a care in the world, said something that sounded like a complete sentence. All morning long, I had been occasionally nodding at him at regular intervals or saying, "That's nice, son," appearing to listen when I really wasn't. To tell you the truth, my mind had drifted off to golf courses unknown. But at one interval it drifted back just in time to hear "and kitty was all sticky, Daddy."

Now a sentence like that can make the hair on the back of your neck stand at attention. *Sticky kitty?* Those two words could have a myriad of meanings, so I stopped, turned to face him, then calmly asked him to repeat the last thing he'd said.

"What about the kitty?" I asked.

I waited for his answer. Talk about a lesson in futility. Children rarely listen to themselves, so asking one to hit the rewind button in his brain is like asking a Border collie to program your VCR. (They can do it, but their timing is all off due to the dog-years factor). So I helped my son retrace his verbal steps.

"It sounded like you said 'sticky kitty.' What about the sticky kitty?" I pressed.

"Sticky kitty?"

It's the confused look on his little mug that always makes me laugh. It's a lot like the look a politician gets when a reporter reminds him of something contradictory he had said a week earlier. Had my son been quicker on his feet—and bilingual—he would have thrown out a "No comprende, Padre."

I had no other choice but to continue with my fatherly interrogation.

"What about the kitty?"

"I had to," he said.

Don't you just love that? Everything a child does is a "had to." There is never any other choice. So I delved into the matter a little further: "What did you 'have to' do?" I asked.

"I had to pour milk all over the kitty," he said, satisfied the inquisition would finally be over. But I couldn't close out the case just yet. I was becoming far too intrigued at this point. And besides, because the kitty was nowhere in sight, it was probably good to get to the bottom of this matter. It was hot, and the kitty's fur could be curdling at that very moment.

I put down the hammer I was pretending to use and continued my line of questioning. You see, while adults do stupid things for absolutely no reason whatsoever, small children usually have very sound reasons for everything they do. It's toddler logic. You just have to keep pressing, and they'll eventually explain themselves. So I kept pressing.

"Why did you 'have to' pour milk all over the kitty?"

"Because he was hot and thirsty," Ryan said, smiling proudly, then returned to his work on his bench. I, on the other hand, still had a few follow-up questions.

"Why did you pour the milk on the kitty and not in his bowl?"

Without hesitation he said, "Because kitty likes to lick himself."

Now, I have to tell you, it took a few seconds for that to make sense to me. But then the light went on in my head. Kitty was hot and thirsty, and he likes to lick himself. Hence, it was my son's way of delivering the milk. It makes sense in a three-year-old kind of way.

So now I'm stuck figuring out how—and whether I should—punish logic like that? The cat may have wanted to punish my son, but I had to admire my kid's resourcefulness. I did suggest to him that in the future he might want to run any new ideas about feeding the household pets by his mother or me beforehand. He assured me that he would. Then we both went back to pretending to be busy.

I have told you all of this to illustrate that listening to those you love is not always easy. Sometimes you hear what you don't want to hear. That is why some have called listening the ultimate act of love.

Since that day, I have tried to work a little harder at being a good listener. But I'm still learning. Daily.

When Ryan was ten, I was driving him to one of his soccer games and heard another one of those lines that make my neck hair stand up. Now, you would think I'd learned my lesson from the sticky kitty incident, but I didn't. I was once again visiting faraway golf ranges in my mind and not paying much attention to his chattering away in the seat next to me, when I happened to hear the words *Dad* and *God* in the same sentence. That will usually make a father sit up and give his child his undivided attention. After all, you don't know if he's praying to God for you, complaining to God about you, or using the Lord's name in vain and needs correcting. So I figured I should pay attention.

"Well, Dad?" he said, awaiting my answer to (for my part) an unknown question.

"What was that?" I asked, hoping he'd repeat himself without my having to confess my wandering attention.

"Does God know what I'm going to be when I get bigger?"

Not really giving it a whole lot of thought, I said, "Yeah, son, I believe He does. He created each one of us with a purpose. So yes, He knows."

My answer seemed to satisfy him.

"OK," he nodded.

He was quiet for awhile, then . . . . "Dad?"

"Yes, son?"

"Is there paper in heaven?"

Again, not really knowing where he was going with this particular line of questioning, I said, "If there's a need for paper, I'm sure God will provide it."

"OK."

Ryan got pensive for a moment. It took awhile for the more laid-back part of my brain to catch up with the frontal lobe and realize there was something a little deeper on his mind. I asked him a question: "What are you thinking about, son?"

He continued to look out the window, then, as if he were talking to the sky, he said, "I don't know. I guess I was just wondering if someone came into my school and shot me dead, when I got to heaven would God be able to write out on paper all the things that I was going to be when I got big."

Wow. I need to repeat that. *Wow.* In all the conversations that I've had with my sons, this one continues to have the most profound effect on me. This was around the time of the Jonesboro, Arkansas, school shootings. I'm sure my son and every school-age kid in America had a lot on their minds during those dark hours.

As a rule, bystanders don't like to think about tragic things like this in depth. We turn the channel on our television sets or turn off the car radio. In the Jonesboro and Columbine shootings, I never allowed myself to empathize too much with the victims and their families. The whole subject was too painful to even think about, so I wouldn't allow my mind to go there. I felt grief for them, but not on a deep level—not on the only level where true empathy lives—in the soul.

Tami absorbs herself in life, taking the painful right along with the good, and so she cried for days, thinking what it must have been like to be a parent of one the victims. She would ask me, as she reached for another tissue, "Can you imagine what it must be like for those parents?"

"Yeah," I would reply, closely guarding that vulnerable side of me. Then I'd open another piece of junk mail. I thought if I ignored the painful reality of the situation or at least shielded myself from it, it would somehow make me stronger than she was.

But Ryan's question wouldn't let me ignore it. Children have a way of bringing us to places where we don't want to go. While we're trying our hardest to properly raise them, they're propelling us into our own maturity. It's almost as if God used Ryan that day to tell me that it was time to start really seeing the events of life. It was time to shed some of my bystander ways and begin my journey to becoming one of life's participants.

I pulled over to the side of the road and just looked at Ryan. I don't think he even realized that his words had affected me so much. I was overwhelmed by a tremendous sense of loss and grief for this generation of kids that even has to think about such things.

For a brief moment, an image of Ryan meeting with a tragic end flashed in my mind. It wasn't a vision or anything spiritual like that. It was just a parent's fears seeming all too real. That was all it took to open the floodgates of my soul. The part of me I had been so good at protecting and hiding through my humor suddenly burst open. I broke down and wept, not just for me and for him, but for all the parents who have lost children in these violent times and for the rest of our youth who have lost their childhoods.

I am so thankful that I heard what a ten-year-old was thinking about on his way to the soccer field. I answered him as best I could, but I don't think I was totally honest with him that day. I told him that he didn't have to worry about all that because I wasn't about to let anything bad happen to him. I didn't want him to worry. But who am I? I'm just his dad. I'm not a superhero. I can't be with him twenty-four hours a day. I can't even be 100 percent sure that I can protect him when he's in my own car. No matter how safely I'm driving, another driver can pull out in front of us and put both our lives in jeopardy. We live in an imperfect world, and so much of what happens in life is out of our control. But how could I tell him that? All he needed at that moment was a hug from his dad and the reassurance that he was going to be all right.

Kids and their questions, huh? It makes me wonder how much of what our kids are saying is going unheard while we selectively listen.

I continue to learn the importance of listening to those we love. But we're busy, the television is blaring, and there are a dozen other things we need to be doing. It's easy to tune them out. Especially for bystanders. We see their lips moving, and we tell ourselves that whatever they have to say we've heard a thousand times. We hope that kind of thinking will get us off the hook. It doesn't. My wife has heard about my athletic youth over and over again, but she still listens anyway. She'll sit and listen to my latest golf tale as if it really matters to her. To me, that's love—the kind of love that requires involvement.

If we listen only when it's convenient, who knows what we might be missing? And let's be honest: it's never convenient. There will always be things to do, places to go, and favorite television programs to watch.

Maybe all of us should take our cue from our heavenly Father who tunes in to us twenty-four/seven. We don't get a halfhearted "uh-huh" when we tell Him about our day. He hangs on every word we utter. Maybe that's why the Bible tells us to pray without ceasing. God really does enjoy hearing from us. Even when we have doubts. Even when we're discouraged.

Even when we're angry. And even when we ask those seemingly unanswerable questions.

I wonder how many times we've made the hair on the back of His neck stand up.

"Anyone who has ears should listen!"
Matthew 11:15

CHAPTER FOUR

I Am Not a Frown Face!

I have spent the better part of my life traveling. Not the kind of traveling most people think of when they picture an entertainer journeying from one place to another—you know, first class, limousines, "Your every wish is our command, Mr. Allen."
I'm talking *my* level of celebrity. I'm talking a working comic without his own sitcom. I'm talking Greyhound.
I once rode the "dog" for three consecutive months. Then I finally arrived at my destination. If I ever make the big time, I envision them taping off that seat on the bus someday and posting a sign that says "Jeff Allen slept here."

But while I await that honor, I'll continue with this missive.

It's been my experience that traveling by bus in America is not something one should plan willy-nilly because it requires a huge commitment of time. I'm not sure, but it seems that whoever is in charge of routing might have failed geometry, or at the very least, was absent the day they covered the concept of the shortest distance between two points being a straight line.

At one point on my three-month journey, I bought a map to help me figure out where in the world I was. It didn't take long to discover that my purchase was a huge waste of money. Apparently, Atlas himself had never heard of the cities we were passing through. I found out later that my bus driver was using Lewis and Clark's original map to route the trip.

If you're getting the idea that it wasn't a fun trip, I'd say you're pretty sharp. We would pull into towns where people would actually line the streets, chanting, "Welcome, Big Iron Horse!" Then they would have a ceremony bestowing the key to the city upon our driver. I thought the honor was due to the skilled way in which he handled the bus over such rugged terrain, but it was just so he could lock up the town as we left. Some of these places were so small, they had to correct the population sign as the bus pulled away, carrying more stowaways desperate to leave the town.

Aside from taking me to faraway places with strange names like Accident, Maryland, and Nowhere, Colorado, there is another thing that I don't understand about bus companies. Why haven't they, in this litigious society, installed seat belts on their buses? Are they figuring that after so many days on a bus, if the driver stops suddenly, the passengers will just stick to their seats anyway? I believe it's referred to as the Human Velcro theory and has something to do with sweat and centrifugal force.

But sweating is the only onboard entertainment on a bus. And believe me, there are plenty of reasons to sweat. The main reason is sometimes sitting about two rows up in the form of an escaped convict. Thanks to him and some other people I have encountered on the roadways, I have learned the skill of sleeping with one eye open, dreaming the big dream while simultaneously watching the budding young serial killer across the aisle.

I don't want to say that my entire busing experience was negative for me. Truth is, contrary to airplanes, buses can pull into every bus station from Los Angeles to Bangor and give their passengers a chance to get out and stretch their legs. It takes a few minutes for the passengers to peel themselves off the seats, but once they're free, they can walk into the terminal and pretend they don't smell half as bad as their fellow passengers. I've often used these stops to take a nice sponge bath in the restroom sink, even blow-drying my hair with the hand dryer. It's not very comfortable, but it counts. And bus station restrooms have all those great toiletries in dispensers. One twenty-five-cent spritz of Brut and I'm good to go.

If you're wondering why bus station restrooms offer these fragrance machines, I would venture to say it's in case a gentleman happens to meet Ms. Right whilst tooling along our nation's roadways. For a quarter of a dollar, he can buy a razor and shave his four-day beard. Another twenty-five cents will garner him the aftershave of his choice, and one more quarter will buy a press-on Yale tattoo so he can impress all the ladies on the bus.

I, however, had no intention of charming anyone on my road trip but did want to cover the bus aroma I was sporting, so I happily inserted my quarter and gained my prize. Problem was, there was so much sweat on my face from the broken air-conditioning system in the terminal that the cologne just beaded up and slid down my cheeks, down my shirt, and came to rest in my navel. This, I believe, explains why we gather lint in our navels in the first place. It's so that, at a time like this, we can make a little wet wipe out of the lint and cologne and freshen our weary faces. It's just a theory, but I believe God has provided us with tools to aid us in any situation; it's simply up to us to discover them. The navel-lint wet wipe could be one of these tools.

But I digress.

I wasn't married at that point in my life, but I did have a girlfriend, which leads me to the biggest advantage to riding the bus—the gift shop at the terminal. Does anything say "I love you" more convincingly than a pewter bus charm? Despite what you think, the charm and the accompanying necklace were very well crafted. They lasted a full two weeks. That may not sound like much to you, but it was one week longer than the relationship lasted.

For my first fifteen or sixteen years of doing stand-up, I was on the road for about forty or fifty weeks each year. I was traveling to comedy clubs around the country, and most of that time, I rode the bus system. Eventually I moved up to what they call a "headliner," and after so many years of leaving the driving to someone else, I finally started flying to my gigs.

As I am sure you are aware, the airline industry has gone through a lot of changes over the years. I can remember when there was hardly any competition, back when the government regulated airfares. You paid a lot more for your ticket then, but the meal was a little more substantial than the peanuts and pretzels they throw at you now. The downside was that people were allowed to smoke on airplanes, and on a long flight, that could be pretty miserable. For us nonsmokers, it was like flying inside an exhaust pipe. I may have had to keep one eye open while riding the bus, but at least I could breathe.

I remember one particular airline called the People's Express. It was the original no-frills airline. I don't think they even had seats. Each of us just stood there and held onto our own subway strap. It's true—you really do get what you pay for. But I could fly from Pittsburgh to Newark for only nineteen dollars. That's right, nineteen bucks. Why was I going to Newark? Did I have business there? Did I have relatives? Did I mention it was only nineteen bucks?

It wasn't until I landed in Newark that I realized I really didn't have anywhere to go in Newark. I didn't know anybody in that town, nor did I know any particular thing to do in Newark. What does one do in Newark? It's not one of the Seven Wonders of the World. It's not even one of the seven mediocrities of the world.

I did finally discover one thing to do in Newark, though. Something I couldn't really do anywhere else—watch a bridge melt. Yes, I had somehow timed my visit perfectly to see one of their highway bridges have a meltdown. Unbeknownst to me, I happened to visit at the precise time the city's garbage (which had been burning under the freeway—cause unknown) suddenly intensified and torched the bridge. Only in Newark could garbage burn for months and no one notice. Actually, it wasn't until the garbage stopped burning that someone finally said, "Hey, what's that smell?"

He was, of course, referring to the strange aroma of fresh air.

The hub of the People's Express airline happened to be in Newark, which could explain why they were a short-lived airline. They should have stayed in business, though, because they did a lot of cool things that separated them from the mainstream carriers.

For instance, they collected your ticket fare after the plane was airborne. They would wheel a credit-card machine down the aisle and start collecting fares as you climbed to ten thousand, twenty thousand, and thirty thousand feet. This might explain the parachute they handed you as soon as you boarded. If you didn't pay, the flight down was free.

Even though I spend a lot of time on airplanes, I don't really enjoy air travel. Especially if I don't get a seat I like. My preference is a window seat. Bystanders love window seats, except the ones in the emergency rows, of course. Emergency rows are no place for a bystander.

When I was a boy, my number one goal on long car trips with the family was to get a window seat and fall asleep before we backed out of the driveway. That meant I could go along on the trip but didn't really have to be involved. Of course, being the youngest of four siblings, I rarely got the window seat. Instead, I had to learn to sleep on the hump in the middle of the seat. This is why to this day I have an aversion to the center seat on airplanes. Just give me a window seat and let me fall asleep before they back the plane out of the gate, and I'm a happy, happy man. But we don't always get what we want out of life, do we?

There was this one particular airline whose name I won't mention, but let's just say they do a lot of traveling in the SOUTHWESTern part of the United States. They apparently haven't figured out the difficult task of assigning seats. What they do is assign their seating on a first-come, first-serve basis, which means that people get their sleeping bags out and start lining up forty-eight hours in advance, like it's a rock concert.

I am sorry, but I am not going to stoop to that kind of juvenile and desperate behavior just to get the seat of my choice. I simply take the plastic paddle (indicating which group of cattle I'm to be called in) they give me and start bopping people over the head with it until I work up to the front of the line and get my window seat. Another man I know does this trick of coughing, sneezing, and groaning that he's burning up with fever as people walk down the aisle toward his row. His SARS impersonation is so good, no one takes a seat within eight rows of him. Now that's genius.

Even if I am lucky enough to get my window seat, I'm finding it increasingly difficult to fall asleep on airplanes. Or maybe I should say "stay" asleep.

One particular flight stands out in my mind. Like most occurrences in my life, it happened while I was just sitting there, minding my own business.

"Hi, everybody. I'm Russell!" the voice boomed across the public address system.

The greeting startled me because I happened to be sitting directly under a speaker. Now, I completely understand the need for perky flight attendants. But at 6:00 A.M. there should be a moratorium on perk. Just give it a couple hours before you start singing Broadway tunes to a captive audience. But Russell was too perky to wait. He was a booming, happy, and I mean happy, happy man.

If you are detecting that Russell and I did not hit it off, your detection devices are operating correctly. Still, I'm a reasonable sort of fellow. I could have forgiven Russell for the Broadway tunes and even the perkiness. But when he woke me up from my nap simply to put a pillow under my head so "I could sleep better," he crossed the line. I inquired as to why he would be touching me at all, and Russell's reply was that I looked uncomfortable. Uncomfortable? I was sound asleep with drool coming down the side of my mouth. What more signs of comfort did my new best friend Russell need?

"Sir," I said, "if you are looking at someone and his eyes are closed and spit is dripping out the side of his mouth, take my word for it: he is comfortable . . . or dead. Either way, the comfort level is pretty high, so you might want to leave him alone."

Russell looked at me after my tirade and all he said was "Frown Face!" Then he walked away.

That's it? Frown Face! That was the best condemnation Russell had of my bad mood? That's right. That was it. I couldn't make up something like that. "Frown Face" is not in my vocabulary. So after he called me that name, which to a comedian could be considered profanity, he walked away with this smug look on his face. I tried not to let it bother me. I just leaned against the window and tried to go back to sleep, but the more I thought about not being bothered, the more bothered I became. "I am not a frown face!" I said to myself over and over again, my upper lip curling into a snarl. "I am a comedian and a happy, happy man," I growled. I knew my wife would vouch for me, so I leaned over and whispered, "Buttercup?"

"Yes, Frown Face?" she said.

Well, needless to say, it didn't matter how much Russell annoyed me, he and Tami became lifelong friends during that two-hour flight. They were united in their cause—torturing me.

After the nap incident came the announcements about the beverage cart. Three times "Mr. Happy" woke me up to announce that the drink cart was coming down the aisle. This is another thing I don't understand about air travel. Who is the beverage cart announcement for? It can't be for the thirsty people because they would be the ones looking for it. Who, then, is it for? Where could people go at thirty thousand feet that might make them miss the drink cart coming down the aisle? Out on the wing? At some point during the flight are passengers entering the plane, saying, "Hey, I was out on the wing. Where's the beverage cart? What do you mean it's been by three times? Why can't you people make an announcement?!"

And why do pilots feel compelled to act as tour guides? When we flew over the Grand Canyon, our pilot got on the intercom and announced that if we looked on the left side of the aircraft, we would see the Grand Canyon. It just so happens that Tami and I were on the left side, so we had a nice view. That is, until the guy in the aisle seat started climbing over Tami and me, trying to take a picture of the big hole in the ground from some thirty thousand feet up with an eight dollar disposable camera. I don't know if you have ever seen the Grand Canyon from thirty thousand feet, but it loses a lot of its wonder. So all I did was mention to the budding Fellini that unless the camera he was using was connected to a CIA spy satellite, the only picture he was getting was the reflection of my Frown Face in the window. Then I told him to get on his side of the bed, figuratively speaking, of course. All I wanted to do was go back to sleep. The man sighed, settled back in his own seat, then rang the attendant button to report me to Russell.

Before I leave the subject of airline announcements, I'd like to ask why attendants are still doing those seat-belt demonstrations? "The Cheery One" (again, Russell) woke me twice so I could pay attention to the seat belt demonstration. But is there still a need to educate the masses on how to attach and detach a seat belt? Just for argument's sake, let's say you've been living in a cave for the past thirty-five years and have never laid eyes on a seat belt. If, for some reason, you can't put that puzzle together in thirty seconds or less, how did you even get to the airport on time?

It seems ironic that my children and your children all ride school buses without seat belts, but by federal law, not only do we have to have them on jets; they have to be demonstrated. And people must be forced, at threat of a delayed takeoff, to fasten them. Flight attendants even check passengers several times throughout the flight to make sure the belts are still fastened. I think this could be so that if the pilot happens to fall asleep and plows into a mountain at six hundred miles an hour, passengers will be able to say, "Well, it's a good thing I had *this* baby on. With all the burning debris around here, we never would have found our unassigned seats again."

There is one consolation to the seat belt, I suppose. If we do ever die in a plane crash, and we fly on to the next life with a flaming seat strapped to our backside, the wait in line at the pearly gates won't seem nearly so bad in the reclining position. Then, just as we're taking in all of heaven's splendor, God Himself will welcome us and say, "Please move your seats to the upright and locked position."

Of course, with my luck, I'd turn and see Russell standing next to me, saying, "Is that you, Frown Face?" On second thought, that could never happen. They say heaven is a paradise, and that means I'll be able to nap for as long as I want without any interruptions.

"Taking one of the stones there,
he put it under his head and lay down to sleep."
Genesis 28:11 (NIV)

CHAPTER FIVE

So There You Are!

I am a fan of Halloween—the candy, that is. I wasn't raised a Christian, so the only moral issue that ever came up during Halloween was when my mother ate my Snickers bars. I considered it stealing, which would be a violation of one of the Commandments. Her story was that she was just checking my treats to make sure there weren't any razor blades in any of them. She was merely looking out for my health and well-being. A nice alibi, but I have a problem with it. If she was simply looking out for my safety, why didn't she ever check the popcorn balls for razor blades? Popcorn balls—did anyone ever eat those things? The only use I could see for them was in the rough parts of town. If a bully started messing with me, I figured I could whip one at his head and split his skull like a cracked cantaloupe. Or at least knock his mask off. No one was getting my bounty!

The biggest bully of all was my brother Kirk. Trying to sneak past him with a sixty-pound sack of sugar was not easy.

He could smell a Milk Dud from fifty yards away. Kirk always felt entitled to the firstfruits of my Halloween goodies because he was older, bigger, and not afraid to get me in a headlock so tight I couldn't breathe. Then he'd wrestle me to the ground and park his carcass on my cranium. Because breathing is an activity I enjoy, I tried to calmly and clearly explain to him that what he was doing could be considered extortion. That's when he'd punch me and say that if I ever used that word again, he'd split open my skull with a popcorn ball. (After years of therapy, I realize that was just his way of showing me how much he loved me.) Then he'd grab my bag of loot and start scarfing down the sugar fast enough to make his pancreas explode.

This may sound odd, but I miss all that.

The more I think about it, it probably wasn't the candy that made October 31 so much fun. It was the anticipation. Have you noticed that the older we get, the farther apart the anticipations seem to get? Now that I have children of my own, I anticipate their anticipations. What I usually get is disappointed. Kids today don't have the same passion about trick-or-treating we used to have. They don't care enough about excess to chase after the "poundage." People my age know exactly what I am talking about. In our day, trick-or-treating was about how many houses you hit and how many blocks you covered. My kids throw on a mask, walk about two blocks, complain about shin splints, then limp home, whining that it wasn't nearly as much fun as they thought it would be.

One particular Halloween night, that of 1994, is an eve that will live in infamy. Enough time has passed that I can finally talk about it. You see, Tami and I have a statute of limitations on how many years I have to withhold the more embarrassing moments from our lives together. The time has come.

I was just minding my business when I heard, *"Jeffrey, come here quick!"*

I ran into the room as soon as I heard her voice. What could it be? I was teeming with excitement to come to the aid of my buttercup.

"What is it, my pet?" I said.

Wait a minute. I think I just had a Ward-and-June-Cleaver moment there. Let me get back to reality. I'm writing my life story, not the Beav's.

After five minutes of screaming back and forth from upstairs to downstairs, Tami called me into the bedroom and told me we were going to a costume party at the home of a childhood friend of hers. She might as well have said we were going to a spinal tap party, as it would've sounded equally as fun.

Maybe I should give you some background information to fully appreciate my predicament. You see, my wife and I grew up on different sides of the tracks. I grew up in Chicago in a blue-collar neighborhood, while she grew up in Hudson, Ohio, in a blue-blood neighborhood. On Halloween in her neighborhood, they threw Faberge eggs at the houses. I never felt very comfortable in that world. And to be perfectly honest, I never liked many of my wife's friends. I considered them, well, snobs. So being invited to one of their homes for a party didn't hold a whole lot of anticipation for me. What it did hold was a lot of dread. As a matter of fact, I would rather go out trick-or-treating with my kids and come home with shin splints than spend a couple of hours trying to remain civil with Bryce and Tanner (yes, those are their real names).

I should also tell you that my wife normally goes out of her way to keep me from these childhood friends, not out of embarrassment but respect for me and my wishes. I figure that Tami and I have made enough friends after we got married whom we both enjoy, and not one of them thinks that Tami married beneath her. Or at least they're not totally convinced of that.

With that said, and to make a long story longer, I agreed to go, and I promised that I would do my best to not "stir it up" with the gang from Hudson. But there was one condition: Tami couldn't stay more than a couple hours. With our deal in place, we headed off for an evening with the Thurston Howells.

There's no need to go into great detail, but I will say that I did not lob the first verbal dart. Bystanders don't start altercations. We usually just stand back and watch them. The person who started our "little tiff" was Bryce's friend, Skip. (No, that's not his real name. He is an attorney.)

This is how things went down. And down. And d

o

w

n.

Tami dropped me off in the kitchen with a group of guys I had never met, then proceeded into the living room to socialize. (*Socialize* is her word for it. I would use the word *gossip*, but because she is a God-fearing woman and knows that is wrong, I'll say "socialize.")

So while Tami was socializing, I was surrounded by total strangers. I felt as if I was back at my first day of kindergarten. I really just wanted my mommy. Now, most people will say that I'm fairly easy to get along with, but I have always had a problem with type-A personalities (and everyone within a four-mile radius of that home was a type-A). I feel uneasy around type-A personalities because we're so different. I have never been tested for ambition, but if I were to hazard a guess, I'm pretty sure I would be a type Z personality, as in napping Zzzzzzzs. Most bystanders would fall into this category.

All these people were talking shop—mergers, acquisitions, and stocks—and totally ignoring me. That was fine by me because I always can use a good nap. But I was trying to fit in for Tami.

That's when Skippy, Bryce's friend, walked in and asked, "Have you all met Tami's husband, Jeff Allen? He's a circus clown."

Now, I don't need to go into great detail about the differences between a stand up comedian and a circus clown, and I certainly don't wish to offend the circus clowns who might be reading this, but let's just say I found his introduction a bit offensive. I managed to bite my tongue and politely corrected him, clarifying that I am a stand-up comedian, not a circus clown.

"Apples and oranges," he said.

"No," I said, "apples and oranges are inanimate and can't defend themselves, so I will speak for them. What does an apple care if you are too ignorant to know the difference between him and an orange?"

"Like you can ascribe gender to produce."

"Well, yes, I think we can. You have a birth certificate, don't you, Skipster?" I asked with a smile, trying to maintain some decorum. "There is a gender on that, isn't there, you kumquat?", losing said decorum.

Again, I say I didn't start this, and I won't go into detail as to what happened next, but it didn't take long for Tami to tell me it was time to go home. I wasn't disappointed in the least, although it was a little sooner than even I had been hoping for. In fact, we were guests at Bryce's house for a total of eight minutes. Never having been to a costume party before, I would guess that eight minutes is a little on the short side.

I would also guess that Tami's original plans had involved staying a bit longer, but that assumption couldn't be verified because by then she was no longer speaking to me. By the way, a threat of silent treatment is something you'll rarely hear a husband make. What are we going to say? "That's it! I'm never grunting to you again"? Men don't tend to speak a lot in the first place, unless it's about something mundane, then we can talk passionately about it for hours. On a night like this, though, it was probably a good thing that Tami opted to go mute on me.

Tami's mute button automatically turned itself off, though, once we were outside Bryce's house. She went all the way to full volume. There I was, naively rejoicing in my early discharge from the Thurston Howell Prison and trying to calculate whether I still had enough time to join the boys trick-or-treating, when my buttercup's voice broke the silence . . . and the sound barrier.

"I can't believe you couldn't keep your mouth shut for one evening!"

I tried telling her that I didn't start the verbal skirmish with Skippy and the gang, but before I could utter another word, she hit me in the head with a Faberge egg and said, "Button it, Jeff! You acted like a fool in there! That reflects on me, don't you see that? Because you're a fool, I'm a fool by association."

"A fool? I am dressed as a green bean, Tami. Please tell me, what is proper etiquette for a green bean? It's not like I was an apple or an orange; then I would know how to behave."

"What are you talking about?" she said. I didn't have the time or ambition to explain the apples-and-oranges reference, so I merely let her continue.

"I am sick and tired of your obnoxious behavior, Jeff! I can never take you to visit my friends anymore! And that's fine with you, isn't it? You go so out of your way to avoid them that most of them think I just made you up!"

I should mention that when my usually calm and understanding wife is down to her last nerve, she has a habit of forgetting that she is talking to another person and at some point begins talking to herself. And so she did.

"That's what they say — 'Poor Tami had to make up a husband because no one would have her.' They probably think I rent the kids to keep up the fantasy. Well, I'm not going to take it anymore!"

It was at this point that I thought I should interrupt her monologue and say something nice. "You're a beautiful woman, Tami. No one in his right mind would think you had to make up a husband and kids."

And I meant that.

"Are you talking? I thought I told you to can it? Didn't I tell you I'm not speaking to you anymore?"

I just sat there quietly and let her continue to vent. And yes, I know it's not polite to eavesdrop on someone talking to herself, but I couldn't help it. Most of her comments were about me, and none of them were very flattering. If I'm ever going to improve, I need this kind of feedback. I didn't need it all at once, but I listened. I wasn't selectively listening either. I listened to everything my wife was saying.

Finally, I had heard enough and simply had to cut in. "I am not going to take anymore of this abuse from a cucumber!"

I said, of course, referring to her cucumber costume. "So, chill, dill!"

Being a stand-up comedian and not a circus clown, I figured the dill reference would make her chuckle. But sometimes I am wrong about these things.

By now a crowd had gathered to watch the two vegetables have it out on Bryce's porch. I have to admit, I was impressed at how quickly those type-A's adopted my bystander mentality. They seemed to enjoy just standing there, watching Tami and me go at it.

Unfortunately, Tami and I started playing to our audience. Playing to an audience will almost always get in the way of better judgment. So, before she could say another thing, I said, "That's it! I'm walking home! I am not riding in the same car with you!"

In my mind, I could hear the crowd cheer. Even Bryce. In reality, though, they just looked at me. But that was OK. I had finally taken a stand. I had finally showed her who was in charge. I had also showed her what a moron I could be, but this green bean had had enough. Even in my bean suit, I was hanging on to what dignity I had left.

As it turned out, I needed that dignity for the long walk home. It was more than five miles (that's thirty-five in green-bean miles). It wasn't going to be easy.

You'd think that my beloved, knowing how far I was going to have to walk, would have felt a little guilty, at least enough for her to say, "Don't be ridiculous, sweetie. Get in the car and we'll discuss this like rational veget—. . . I mean, adults."

But instead, what came out was, "OK, good, because I don't want to share the same space with you either right now!"

With that, Tami drove off and I walked home.

All the way home I kept asking myself how in the world a bystander like me let it get to this point. The entire scene went entirely against the bystander credo.

At one point I tried to hitchhike, but trust me, no one is picking up green beans in this country anymore. Some people pulled over just long enough to get within earshot, then yelled, "HEY! What's it like in the valley? HO, HO, HO!" By the fifth car, you'd think I would have seen it coming, but I fell for it no fewer than seven times in the ninety minutes spent walking home.

When I finally arrived at our house, I opened the door and walked up the stairs to the bedroom. Tami was sitting in bed, obviously waiting for me. I know this because when she saw me, she said, "So there you are!"

So there I are? That's all she had to say? And she had said it as though we had been playing a game of hide-and-seek. Had she forgotten that I had just walked all the way home? I started to stoop to sarcasm and ask if she thought I had been in the basement playing Ping-Pong all this time, but my green-bean feet were killing me. All I wanted to do was get out of that stupid costume and go to bed.

I decided to simply ignore my wife and not reply. If she wanted to play her little game, I didn't have to participate. I was going to go to sleep. But as I walked by our bathroom mirror, I caught a glimpse of how ridiculous I looked, and my pride started to soften just a bit. I didn't like fighting with my buttercup. I wanted to call a truce. And we did.

So who was to blame for this disaster of an evening? I'll accept responsibility for the fiasco with my wife's friends (although Skip really started it), but the costume idea was Tami's. If she hadn't insisted on being talking vegetables long before Big Idea ever got the big idea for that sort of thing, the situation wouldn't have gotten so far out of hand. A husband and wife arguing on a front porch doesn't draw nearly as large a crowd as a cucumber and green bean can. Without those costumes, people would have just gone on with their own lives and ignored us. And if we hadn't had the audience, I never would have grandstanded and suggested walking home. Bystanders don't make grandstands. And we certainly don't walk home. That would be considered exercise. That's another thing this bystander doesn't do. When Aaron was a baby, my wife and I bought an exercise bike, and in three years, we've only put five miles on it. Most of that was from the baby just spinning the wheels.

When you get down to it, I suppose the bulk of the blame lies with anticipation. My wife anticipated having an unreasonable amount of fun at the party with her friends, while I anticipated misery. She had set her sites higher than what we knew would probably happen, and I had made sure that the bad time I had been anticipating came true. Subconsciously, we both had sabotaged the evening.

Anticipation can be good or undermining. We can anticipate that first day of summer vacation, the goodies we're going to bring home from trick-or-treating, the fun time we'll have dining out with our family, or the horrible time we're going to have at a party with our spouse's friends.

But when all is said and done, we still have to accept and live in reality. If something goes wrong, we can adapt. If the restaurant loses our reservation, we can adapt. If our vacation plans fall through, we can adapt. And when we end up making fools out of ourselves in a green-bean costume, we can learn from the experience and move on, knowing that God, and the cucumber we love, will forgive us.

"Better a meal of vegetables where there is love than a fattened calf with hatred."
Proverbs 15:17

CHAPTER SIX

I Am a Man!

"It's the man's job!"

Tami says this as a last resort to get me to do the things that I don't want to do. These chores are apparently noted on some invisible honey-do list she carries around in her head. I've never seen this list, but I know it exists and is always available to her whenever she needs it.

"It's the man's job!"

Those four simple words have the power to get even a bystander like me to spring into action. Every time Tami plays this testosterone card, I fall for it. It feels good to be the man — to reign on my recliner/throne until I'm summoned to save my family and quite possibly the world yet again. It's a real ego-feeder.

This ploy of hers has worked for as long as we've been married. I tried the reverse on her one time. I suggested that cooking was the woman's job. As soon as I regained consciousness, I apologized for that thoughtless remark. Women want the freedom to decide for themselves exactly what the woman's job is. And I can't say I blame them.

Who says the traditional jobs of their mothers have to be passed down to them?

But as for the man, some of his jobs have been etched in stone for centuries. I'd like to challenge a few of these duties. For one thing, who said men should mow the lawn? I don't enjoy yard work. The only reason I mow the grass at all is to look for golf balls. And who says the man should be the fixer of plumbing? I don't know anything about a stopped-up sink. I know a snake is involved, but I don't have a clue as to whether it should be venomous or not. Still, whenever the lawn needs a shave or the sink won't drain, I am called into action once again by those four little words, "It's the man's job."

And off I go. I leave my throne and defend my castle. To tell you the truth, I don't know what bothers me more: the fact that she thinks I'm dumb enough to fall for this year in and year out or the fact that I am dumb enough to fall for this year in and year out.

The undisputed topper on this list of men's jobs is checking out strange noises in the middle of the night. This has, and probably always will be, considered a man's job. I'm sure this is due somewhat to the potential danger involved, but I have a question. What about those of us who know our wives are braver than we are and aren't ashamed to admit it? In a situation like this, shouldn't the lead defender be the one with the most courage?

I married a tough woman—beautiful, but tough. The first thing she did when we got married was to take my spine away from me. I think she was afraid I'd hurt myself with it. Not that I've minded her actions. A spine is something a bystander doesn't have a lot of use for. And anyway, it's not like she gave it away to Goodwill or anything like that. She keeps it in her purse and returns it to me whenever I have to do something manly. Living in the suburbs as we do, that isn't all that often. The most dangerous thing we've encountered out here was a drive-by taunting by some of the neighborhood kids. (They made fun of my shoes as I was standing on the driveway making a phone call. Hoodlums.)

But there have been plenty of times when I've had to step up as the man of the house in the wee hours of the morning. Every husband can relate to this. My wife will wake me up to say she heard a noise downstairs in the basement. I open one eye and give her my manly answer: "So?"

"So, here's your spine," she'll say, handing it back to me.

"For what?" I ask, not really expecting an answer.

"I heard something. Go check it out."

Now, first of all, I say if she's the one who heard a noise, she should be the one to get out of bed and check it out. Furthermore, if she had been sleeping, like she should have been doing, she wouldn't have heard the noise. I know this because I *was* sleeping and didn't hear any noise. So I usually tell her that if she'd just go back to sleep, she won't hear it again.

As you can see, bystanders and strange noises in the middle of the night don't mix. If a burglar was indeed in my house stealing my VCR, what am I, a charter member of the Bystander Club, going to do about it? Stand there in my underwear and tell him a few jokes? I'm going to do what all bystanders do. I'm going to let him have the VCR. What do they cost now anyway? About nine bucks? I can postpone buying a new suit and buy another video player, no problem.

I AM A MAN!

But even a bystander has to see combat sometimes. I had to one night back in 1996, but thankfully, I've lived to tell about it.

It was late and there was a crash in the basement. Immediately, I took the action common to every bystander: I rolled over and started to go back to sleep. After hearing a second crash, I knew I had to take another course of action. I woke my wife up and told her I'd heard a noise downstairs. Her reply sounded vaguely familiar. "So?" she said.

I knew I wouldn't be able to get back to sleep until I checked out the strange noise. My imagination and my wife would never allow it. I pictured the worst, of course. Who knew what kind of confrontation I was in for? I secretly wished I could have asked Tami to go with me. Yes, I'm the man, but as I said, Tami's tough. If the intruder tracked mud on her new rug, she'd send him flying back to where he came from without even breaking a sweat. I haven't had the tests done yet, but I think I might be allergic to danger.

Despite my fears, I knew I was going to have to face this burglar myself. I also knew I was going to need my spine back for this one. While Tami pondered the ramifications of trusting me with it again, there was yet another crash. We both heard this one, so the mood immediately turned serious. We decided that I needed something stronger than just my presence (even with a spine) down in the basement. I looked around for some kind of weapon to take along with me for added security and protection.

Now, when it comes to actual weapons other than my wit, I'm out of luck. (Sometimes even with my wit, I'm outgunned.) But this situation called for serious backup. Or whatever I could find in the dark quickly. I found the twelve-gauge shotgun my father had given me years ago, only the firing pin was broken. He had told me if I'd get it fixed, it'd be a good gun for me. Of course, in the true bystander tradition, I never got it fixed. I've easily made forty-five mental notes over the years to get it fixed, but they dislodged from my brain and are floating around somewhere in my system. This is where most of my mental notes end up.

But with a stranger surely in my basement, I grabbed the shotgun anyway. My theory was, if I get face-to-face with the crook, I could use the gun to hold him at bay until the police arrive. What thief is going to look down the barrel of a twelve-gauge and say, "You know, I'm only guessing, but I'll bet you that firing pin is busted"?

Another plus to attacking with even an impotent weapon is that if the bad guy gets it away from you, you'll get the last laugh.

With broken weapon in hand, I started the descent to our basement. Every man reading this knows that at this point in the scenario, my heart started racing and my adrenaline was surging. I was defending my domain. Even in the face of danger, it does give you a bit of a rush. Step by step, inch by inch, I was coming closer to my fate. My heart was pounding so hard, I could scarcely breathe. By the time I reached the basement, I was pumped and ready to flip on the light switch and give that intruder a taste of Jeff justice. He would be sorry he picked my home to invade. It may take awhile for a bystander to get started, but once he's pumped, he's a force to be reckoned with.

I steadied my gun and turned on the switch. As I quickly scanned every corner of the basement, searching for the nocturnal invader over the top of my twelve-gauge, I heard my wife yell from the top of the basement stairs, "What are you doing, Jeff?! You know that gun doesn't work!"

If there *had* been someone down there, he probably would have turned himself in just out of pity for me. The noise turned out to be nothing more than some boxes losing their balance, but even so, I ended up getting far more than humiliation out of that night. I learned something very important: to keep my family safe, I needed a different plan than the one I had. I needed a plan that was panic-proof—something that could not be sabotaged from afar, would fit my bystander lifestyle, and would not involve a broken shotgun. I was going to need what all good crime-fighters need.

That's right. A uniform! Now whenever I hear a noise in the night, I put on the Noise Uniform. The Noise Uniform is nothing more than Tami's bathrobe and big fuzzy slippers, but my theory is that if a bad guy is ever hiding out in my basement for real, he'll take one look at me in my uniform, freak out, and say, "Wow, if you're the woman of the house, I don't even wanna meet the man who married you! That guy's been punished enough for one lifetime! Here's your VCR back!"

Granted, it's a theory, but I sleep much better now, knowing that I have a plan in place. And as with all good plans, it's already been field-tested. Once, anyway. I believe I was on my third nap, and Tami was in the kitchen washing something. I was just about to tee off in the Chrysler Classic when I was awakened from my slumber by a bloodcurdling scream from the kitchen. I immediately recognized the scream as belonging to my very own damsel in distress. Now, they say a man isn't truly alive until he finds something more valuable than his own life—something worth dying for. I never had this in my life until I met my wife. She was the first person I truly fell in love with. She captured my heart. Later on, it was my children, and finally, Jesus Christ. Now I have a bunch of people worth dying for, and as ironic as that seems, I am more alive today than I ever was.

But saying you're willing to die for someone and actually being called upon to do so are different matters altogether. Few of us are ever required to prove a claim like that. But on this particular night, I was being asked to prove it. I had to put my life in peril for my very own buttercup.

It all began with that aforementioned scream.

"Ahhhhhhhhhhhhh!"

It took me a few seconds to get my bearings straight, but when I finally got focused, I realized I had no time to put on the "uniform." That was my first mistake. I immediately grabbed my rifle (a new one) and headed toward the kitchen. What I saw there horrified me. The love of my life was standing on a chair, wide-eyed and hyperventilating, trying with all her might to scream again, but nothing was coming out. I looked around for the monster, the horrible villain, the frightening sight that was the cause of such terror. After all, standing on chairs isn't something my wife does on a regular basis. But I didn't see anything.

"Tami! What is it?!" I asked.

All she could do was gasp for air (I think she sucked in part of the drapes) and point at the floor. Another *"ahhhhhhhhhhhhh!"* finally escaped her, then she was speechless again and pointed toward the floor. He must have been a very short burglar. She pointed again. That's when I saw it. It was moving along the floor with eight legs of sheer horror! The largest daddy longlegs ever to creep this earth. This thing had a small puppy in its teeth. Or a bagel crumb . . . I'm not sure which. All I know is that I was suddenly thrust face-to-face with the opportunity to prove my love to buttercup. Both adrenaline and testosterone were rushing through my veins. I felt chest hair sprouting, and my voice dropped a few octaves as I told Tami to stand back. With the stealth of a Mafia hit man, I raised my rifle, pointed it right at the arachnid's eyes, and squeezed off what I thought would be the fatal shot.

But the BB just knocked the crumb out of his mouth. I didn't have time to repump my Daisy rifle, so it looked like I would have to take on the beast in hand-to-hand combat. Mano a mano. Two legs versus eight.

I dropped the gun and went after our intruder with a vengeance. It would be the mother of all exterminations. But just as I started my ground warfare with an all-out Nike assault, Tami found her voice and tried to call me back.

"Oooooh, don't kill it," she pleaded.

Don't kill it? What was she thinking? Of course my plan was to kill it. This was no time for me to retreat. That arachnid had to pay for terrorizing my loved one and disturbing my peace. Did she think I would just get the spider in a half nelson and run him outside? I don't think so. I am a bystander, but I am no wimp! I investigate strange noises in the middle of the night. I am the spider annihilator of my home! I am the defender of my buttercup! I AM A MAN!

"Prepare to meet your Maker, bagel thief!" I screamed as I lifted my foot and aimed the kick that would end this nightmare. But as I began to bring my foot down, I caught a glimpse into his little eyes. For the first time, I saw another side of this eight-legged beast—his softer side. He wasn't a bagel thief at all. He was just misunderstood. Maybe he was looking out for his family just as I was looking out for mine. Maybe he was a bystander in life, just trying to go about his day and stay out of everyone else's way. Maybe he had moved into that house long before we did. Maybe I was the intruder. And now there he sat, looking up at the sole of my shoe, pleading with his eyes for me not to end his life. Looking at him (not at his fangs, but at his heart), I could see him for who he really was—just a regular Joe, out hunting for food to bring to his kids. I began to see our similarities rather than our differences. It was moving me to a place inside myself that I had never wanted to see before—my sensitive side. There was a war going on inside me. All this took place in a matter of seconds.

I was so moved I started to drop to my knees to beg his forgiveness, but just as I felt myself going down, I saw him laugh. Not a big laugh, but an ever-so-slight smirk. If I'd had a camera, I would have captured that look and put it on the Internet. I knew that smirk. I've seen it a lot at my concerts. It brought me back to reality, and I realized what was really happening. I was being manipulated by all the bleeding-heart liberal media types that had brainwashed me since I was a kid. Not this time, Al Franken. Or maybe it was the right-wing conspiracy. Or . . .

No, this was just between him and me! That bug was history! He was going to that big web in the sky or down the toilet. I said, "Sayonara, Eight Legs!" then kung fu-ed him with all 185 pounds of me.

Looking back on the incident, I'd have to say it was one of my finer moments. A bystander had risen to the occasion and won. But what happened next has perplexed me for years. When I turned to my wife and puckered for my hero's kiss, she said disgustedly, "You didn't have to kill it. Now who's gonna clean up the mess?"

That was it? *Who's gonna clean up the mess?* I saved this woman's life by placing my own in peril, and that's all the credit she was going to give me? I had run to her when she beckoned. I had looked fear in the eyes and faced it head on. I didn't balk. I didn't turn tail and run. I had stood tall in my Nikes, and she couldn't give me the adoration I was due? No wonder I've always preferred to be a bystander. When you're not involved, life doesn't have to make sense.

But I knew in my heart, I had done the right thing. I couldn't let that spider live to smirk again.

I must admit my first reaction was to leave the conquered intruder on the floor right where he was as a warning to any other creepy creatures that might be contemplating similar aggression. My theory was that they would see the carcass and realize there were laws in my house and a system in place to enforce them. That, or they would smell the testosterone heavy in the air and leave the way they came in.

But I did as my wife asked. I cleaned up the carcass with a paper towel. Then, being the mature and considerate husband that I am, I decided to chase my beloved around the house with it. It was the perfect end to another perfect day.

"GROW UP!" Tami screamed as she ran from room to room.

"*Grow up?*" I replied, holding up my kill. "I don't have to! I am a MAN!"

It was fun . . . until she made me give her my spine back.

"One man of you shall chase a thousand."
Joshua 23:10 (NKJV)

CHAPTER SEVEN

Just Because I'm a Moron Doesn't Mean It's My Fault

I want to thank the lawyers of America for saving my life. Had it not been for some past multimillion-dollar liability lawsuit, the warning on my can of shaving cream would not have been there, and I would not have been dutifully forewarned that I could have accidentally killed myself shaving. It's a dangerous world. Even as I write this, I am still visibly shaken from the incident of some weeks ago. For your sakes, and to get the word count up on my book, I will try to remember as many details of that near-fatal morning as I can.

Like most bystanders, I woke up late that fateful day. Bystanders like to wake up late. It makes the day shorter and lowers the risk of having to actually get involved in something. But on this particular day, I did have a full agenda planned. I needed to call the golf course for a tee time, and . . . well, I'm sure I had other things to do as well.

I took a quick shower, dressed, and stopped off at the kitchen for a quick breakfast. It was there that I caught a glimpse of my reflection in the chrome toaster and realized I needed a shave.

Over the years, I have found that if I don't shave by noon, I look like a terrorist. That's not the look I'm going for. I should also mention that if I don't get some nutrition into my system soon after rising, my blood sugar plummets and I actually do become a terrorist. OK, not really, but I do get menacingly whiny.

Being pressed for time, I knew I was going to have to improvise. I decided to kill two birds with one stone by combining my morning shave with my morning meal preparation. I got my shaving cream and razor out of the bathroom, grabbed some bacon and a couple of eggs out of the refrigerator, and made my way to the backyard. The backyard? you ask. Well, yes, of course. I don't prepare my breakfast over the traditional controlled flame of an ordinary kitchen stove. No, no, no. Like so many of you, I prefer to do it over a blazing bonfire in the backyard. In fact, that is one of the primary reasons I moved to the country: to enjoy breakfast bonfires in my backyard without those pesky homeowner associations writing me a citation for my garden inferno. I have found that once the fire really gets going, not only can I fry my eggs in no time at all, but if I need to, I can also burn some of the old furniture that's been cluttering up our basement. Why waste a good fire? I always say.

As I waited for my bonfire to get good and hot (which would be pretty quick because I had, like any good chef, doused it with a gallon or two of gasoline), I decided to get my shave over with. But as I picked up my shaving cream can, I happened to notice its warning label. Well, imagine my surprise when right there on the can I read, "Do not use near fire or flame. Contents will explode under pressure."

Wow! Who would have ever thought this was a concern? Here all along I had been assuming that I could shave while hovering over a bonfire in my backyard and everything would be fine. But apparently, this is a dangerous thing to do. I can only assume that some guy like me, who was probably running late and in need of a little nourishment, tried to shave while standing over a backyard bonfire and is now resting in peace (and pieces) in three different states.

Excuse me, but did all the common sense of the world seep out the hole in the ozone layer when we weren't looking? Why do we have to be reminded about things that we should know instinctively? Shouldn't we know that one should never try to sauté an aerosol can over an open flame? That would seem like a no-brainer to me.

But apparently, it's not. Times have changed. Common sense used to be something that most of us just inherently possessed—standard equipment, if you will. But fewer and fewer people seem to possess common sense anymore, so much so that I fear it may be evaporating from our gene pools.

And that's why we have warning labels.

In my opinion, though, a few of these legal warnings seem to be counterproductive; they can give certain minds certain ideas that might not have occurred there before. I was a child once myself, and I can tell you that had it not been for the warning on that can of my mother's hair spray, I never would have known that it could be turned into a flamethrower. So it's not too much of a stretch to imagine a kid picking up a can of shaving cream and reading, "Contents will explode under pressure," and calling one or two of his adolescent little chums over to see if what it says is really true. Next thing you know, all three young men are holding a lighter and looking curiously at the can of shaving cream that heretofore offered no explosions whatsoever.

"So you think it's true?" says the one holding the can.

"What?"

"This label. It says, 'Do not use near fire or flame. Contents will explode.' You think it's for real?"

"Only one way to find out."

"Yeah, that's what I say."

"You're not gonna try it, are you?" says the bystander of the group.

"It's OK. I'm discovering. You know, like Edison."

The next sound they hear is BOOOOOOOOOOM! as the can explodes.

But unlike Edison, the only thing they've discovered in the process is how far shrapnel can fly and the telephone number for the best attorney in town.

Trip over your shoelaces? Sue the store.

That bowl of hot soup you ordered is too hot? Sue the restaurant.

Cut your arm on a window while breaking into a house? Sue the homeowner.

People don't accept personal responsibility for their actions anymore. Our courts are filled with frivolous lawsuits and ridiculous claims that should have been laughed at instead of pursued throughout our legal system.

Should companies really have to tell us everything we shouldn't do with their products before they are totally free from liability?

"Do not operate car while playing the banjo."

"Do not gargle shampoo."

"Do not use microwave as an aquarium."

"Do not eat mulch."

"Do not tap dance on glass coffee table."

It's not only personal responsibility that's disappearing; fun is too.

I was standing in a Toys "R" Us recently, and everywhere I looked I could see the evidence of lawyers. There was warning label after warning label. This kind of overly cautious behavior can take all the enjoyment out of life. "Operate this toy only under the direct supervision of a legal team" isn't all that enticing to an eight-year-old.

I, for one, happen to be grateful that I grew up in an America where the only thing you got from doing something moronic was stitches and a swat from your old man for being a doofus.

But times have changed. More and more, it seems we're becoming a paranoid society. We're afraid of injury, afraid of each other, and afraid of life.

A couple months ago when I was at my sister's house, I saw my nephew come downstairs, dressed to disarm a nuclear device. Turns out he was only going roller-blading.

Nobody wants to see their children get hurt, but a constant chorus of "Watch out!" creates a certain degree of irrational and overly cautious behavior in the average human being. In our zeal to protect ourselves, we have lost sight of the deepest philosophical statement to come out of my generation: "Stuff Happens." When I was a kid, it was understood that kids did stupid things. That was how we learned *not* to do stupid things. I can't tell you how many times my father told me (after I had done something moronic), "You got exactly what you deserve." Yet if you go by the juries in America, people who burn themselves with hot coffee deserve fully funded retirement accounts, and kids who climb over protective fences to play Frisbee with a lion at the zoo deserve to own the zoo or close it down.

Years ago, there was a commercial that featured a client proudly announcing that a popular law firm had just won him a million dollars in an accident claim. "And I wasn't even injured!" he said, beaming.

Where will it all end?

If you ask me (and I could sense that you wanted to), all this litigation has done is turn up the volume on our whining. There's so much whining going on in America today, I'm surprised that Canada hasn't complained about the noise.

My wife just came in and read what I was writing and told me to stop my whining. She's right. I do a fair share of whining myself, so I will get to the point of this chapter, which is how much the human race likes to blame.

The way I see it, it all started with Adam and Eve.

Adam: The woman YOU made for me, out of my own rib, I might add, gave me the apple.

Eve: The serpent tempted me.

Serpent: Hey, I was only trying to help.

OK, so two of the above were blamers and one was just a deceiver. But it illustrates how blaming others for our own behaviors has been going on since shortly after the world began. So how can we possibly delete a virus that's been that long in the system? The answer is, we can't, at least not totally. But we don't have to continue feeding it either. We blame our parents, our children, our teachers, our pastors, our neighbors, and even God. How many times have we said the following, filling in our own endings?

"Where were You, God, when . . . ?"

"God, if You loved me, You would have . . ."

"I prayed, Lord, so why didn't You . . . ?"

The scenarios are endless, but the complaints are the same. We wonder why God didn't keep us from that car accident—the one where we made that unsafe lane change. We ask where He is when our car payment's overdue, when we know good and well we bought a car that was way over our budget in the first place. We blame God for whatever goes wrong in life and have a tendency to ignore Him when things go right.

Blame: maybe God would like to see us quit passing so much of it around.

But then again, if this book doesn't sell and I can't buy my dream home for my wife and kids, then that really is going to be your fault. Some things are just black and white.

"She fell at his feet and said:
'My lord, let the blame be on me alone.'"
1 Samuel 25:24 (NIV)

CHAPTER EIGHT

What Is Your Problem?

I try to live by the words in the Bible. I don't drive according to the maps in the back of the Bible or anything like that. And to be perfectly honest with you, I've never gotten through all the begats. But the part that was dictated by God seems pretty important to me, so I try to pay attention there.

Somewhere in the New Testament is a particular Scripture I once saw and made a mental note to remember its location. Of course, because my mind regularly deletes these mental notes, I can't tell you where to find the Scripture. (OK, I could but I had to look it up, so you should too.) But it's something about being "slow to anger, quick to listen, and slow to speak." (The "slow to speak" part is what southerners base their accent on.)

The reason I made note of the Scripture (Martha's note: if you're still looking, it's James 1:19) was because it seemed like good advice that I might use someday.

Someday came about eight or ten years ago.

It was that time of night all parents relish — the day is drawing to a close, the dinner dishes are put away, the kids are all bathed and sitting in front of the television watching *The Lion King* for the fourteenth time in one week. (Actually, I don't care if I have to hear those same songs over and over again until my ears start to hemorrhage. As long as it keeps them quiet, I can "Hakuna Matata" with the best of them.)

It was that "ahhhh" time of the evening.

Now, I have learned as a parent not to take anything for granted. The Bible is very clear on this, saying for us to enjoy today because we don't know what tomorrow will bring. In a house with children, it could be changed to "enjoy the minute because you do not know what the next minute will bring."

So there I was, nurturing my children and enjoying the peace and quiet, and I might add, minding my own bystander business, when everything changed in a single moment. I have no idea what evil force compelled my wife to give these sweet children Popsicles, but I do know that you never disturb quiet children with *anything*. Instinctively, Tami knew that too. But like I said, it was the forces of evil (OK, mischievousness) driving her. Unfortunately, I didn't realize we were dealing with this kind of invisible warfare until afterward, when the smoke had cleared and I was able to analyze the horrific scene from beginning to end. But I did finally see it. Hindsight is a great angle to view life from, but only as long as you learn something that will help you in the future. For the record, here is how it all transpired.

"Who wants a Popsicle?" my wife asked, jumping up from the sofa and piercing the silence with her sly temptation. Of course, they all answered, "Not now, Mother. We are being quiet for Father and this will disrupt this moment of serenity that he is experiencing right now."

Sorry. I guess I had a Norman Rockwell moment. Let's get back to real life. What *really* happened was more like the moments after a nearsighted woodpecker knocks on a hornet's nest.

Aaron, the oldest, jumped up, screaming, "I want a red one! I want a red one!"

"There's only one red one," my wife said.

"Then I get it!" he insisted.

"He always gets the red one," Ryan, then nine years old, cried. "Why can't I have it?"

Before my wife could answer, the baby started screaming, "DEEEEN! DEEEEEEN!" Now my wife had to stop and ask Ryan to interpret because he's the only one in the family who speaks fluent two-year-old. According to our translator, the baby desired a green one.

"Let me see if I can find one," Tami answered, looking through the box.

"Get me the red one first," Aaron pressured.

"Why does he get the red one, Mommy?! He always gets the red one!"

"DEEEEN! DEEEEEEEN!" interjected the baby.

"I do not!" Aaron said.

"Do too!" Ryan countered.

"Do not!"

"Do too!"

"Do not!"

"Do too!"

"DEEEEEEEEN! DEEEEEEEEEN!"

I take this brief time out to ask you, the reader, where children learn to argue like this. It never results in a satisfactory end to the argument. It just keeps going and going: do not, do too, do not, do too. It's immature and nitpicky, and if it were possible to bring you into my head during an exchange such as this, you would see each word bouncing off my skull like a racquetball during an intense game. Bam! Bam! Bam! Bam!

So as I was sitting there in my easy chair, actually starting to vibrate from the anxiety that was permeating my entire being (are you beginning to sense a pattern here?), I began to believe that Tami might have interrupted our peace on purpose. Not out of spite. Just mischief. My wife, lovely as she is, has an extremely warped sense of humor. One time she was getting ice cream for the boys. Although her routine is to give each of them one scoop of the exact same size, she thought it would be funny to give it to them in different size bowls. Try explaining to a couple of toddlers that bowl size doesn't matter because they all have the same size scoop. Ready for another game of mental racquetball?

"Daddy, Aaron got more than me!"

"Nuh-uh. Ryan got more."

"Did not."

"Did too."

"Did not."

"Did too."

Finally I decided to triumph with a little Allen logic. I took another bowl from the cupboard and said, "Look, here is a bigger bowl than Aaron's. Now, I'll take your one scoop of ice cream and dump it into this bowl. See, it's a bigger bowl, but it's the same amount of ice cream. Get it?"

"Yeah," he giggled. "I got more than him now."

As long as my children are happy, I'm happy. Of course a minute later, Aaron came strolling in, screaming, "Dad! How come Ryan has more ice cream than me?"

To which I replied, "He does not."

"Does too."

"Does not."

"Does too."

So I got him a bigger bowl and poured his one scoop of ice cream into it. Satisfied, he ran into the living room and began to taunt Ryan, "Ha! Now I have more than you!"

Sure enough, into the kitchen walked Ryan.

"Dad, he's got more than me!"

I realize it's too late to cut this short, but I do need to tell you how it all ended. An hour later, I had both kids eating their one scoop of ice cream out of two separate fifty-five-gallon drums, while my wife sat in her chair, laughing. This whole thing is her idea of funny. So her initiating the Popsicle situation and igniting another Allen family war makes me think she did it on purpose. She, of course, denies this, but I know what I know. As I said, hindsight is a great angle to view life from.

While I'm processing this theory, trying my bystander best not to get sucked into the vortex of what is going on in my living room and not to allow my head to explode from the cacophony of voices ("Red one! Orange one! Deeeeen! Deeeeeeennnn!"), I let my mind wander to an evil thought of my own. If ever I meet the man who came up with the idea for the variety pack of Popsicles (instead of one uniform color of harmony and love), I will beat him into a pulp with Popsicle sticks. Bystanders are not usually vindictive like that, but our nerves do have their limits.

Whoever said variety is the spice of life did not have children. If you have more than one child, variety is the spice of aneurysms. I think someone should come up with a twenty-four pack of clear Popsicles just for us parents and call it the Popsicle Disarmament Pack. I can see my kids even now digging through the box, asking, "What color can I have?"

"Clear," I'll answer. "They're all water-flavored!"

"Nuh-uh."

"Uh-huh."

"Nuh-uh."

"Uh-huh."

Now *that's* my idea of funny.

I have to say that I did hang in there during Tami's entire Popsicle distribution. Whenever I would start to lose it, that Scripture verse about being slow to anger, quick to listen, and slow to speak would pop into my head. So I would wait. I told myself that I . . . was . . . going . . . to . . . be . . . slow . . . to . . . anger. Slow to anger. SLOW TO ANGER!

Finally, I told God that I had, indeed, waited long enough. Five whole minutes had passed. By now, I was due a green light on anger and speaking. My dad wouldn't have put up with such a scene for five seconds, much less five minutes.

But I held my tongue—the blue one, thanks to the blue Popsicle that no one else had wanted. I waited for everything to settle back down. I didn't think a little peace in my home was asking a lot. All I wanted was some quality time with my kids without the bickering, the whining, the immature competitiveness. (A man can dream, can't he?)

It was while I was busy dreaming—or just numb from all the noise—that I heard it. Every father reading this knows what "it" is. "It" is the sound of sibling flesh on sibling flesh. It's usually a prelude to something that sounds like this, "AAAAAAAAAAAAAAAAAAAhhhhhhhhhhhhhhhhhhhh! DAAAAAAAAAd, he hit me!"

He, in this case, was Aaron. Aaron wanted that red Popsicle so bad, he smacked his brother in the face to get it. I have to tell you, when one of my sons screams like that, the kind of scream that could break jelly glasses, it's as if I have a raw nerve cut open and someone is pouring salt on it.

At this point, every hair on my head shot straight out of my skull and stuck in the ceiling like toothpicks at a '50s diner. I jumped up out of my chair and bravely went where every dad has gone before — right in the middle of his pile of offspring — and shouted, "Shuuuuuuuuut uuuuuuuuuuuup!! Will you pleeeeeeaaasseeee, just be quiiiiiiiiiiiiet!"

Every dad reading this also knows the look I got after my Popsicle intervention. Four heads, with these baffled looks on their faces, turned to look at the lunatic in the middle of the room. My wife was the first to speak. "What is your problem?" she said.

"My problem? *My problem?* You wanna know what my problem is?"

And I was ready to tell them. I have to admit, before I reacted to the moment, I hadn't given all that much thought to what Tami would say. But one of the skills that comes from years of being a nightclub comic is the ability to think on your feet. So I continued, "What difference does it make what color it is? For gosh sakes, the baby's two. He doesn't even know his colors yet. Give him a red one and tell him it's green. He can find out you tricked him when he gets into kindergarten — or therapy."

Ryan interrupted, "But I want the red one!" Tears were starting to form in his eyes.

"Oh, for gosh sakes. It's just sugar, water, and food coloring," I said. "Reach in the box, pull one out, and surprise yourself."

We can all guess who the bad guy was at this point. It happens to all of us dads. After making a stand like that, it's one of the longest walks back to your chair you'll ever have to make. It's a bystander's nightmare. I could hear all the sniffles, so I turned around to apologize, but before I could, I noticed that the baby was now holding up an orange Popsicle and grinning from ear to ear.

"Deen."

"That's right, son," I said. "Deen."

Now, you'd think this would be the end of it, wouldn't you? Well, it was . . . for the children. They went back to *The Lion King* and humming "Hakuna Matata." But adults are different. We tend to let things linger a little longer, especially when it's a case of someone needing to apologize. But I wanted to end the matter for all of us. I had no choice. Whenever I feel bad about something, there is this lingering guilt that hangs over my head. My wife, as with most wives, has guilt vision and can see this cloud from miles away. She knew I was hammering myself for how I had reacted over a box of Popsicles, but I also knew how understanding she would be.

She leaned over and said tenderly, "What the heck was that all about, Jeff? I had it under control."

"You did not!"

"Did too!"

"Did not!"

"Did too!"

It was a familiar-sounding fight. But for the life of me, I just don't know where the kids learned all this stuff from, do you?

These days the boys no longer fight over Popsicles. They realize there are more important things to do with their energy. Aaron is in the military now, and Ryan has just a few more years left of high school and then he'll be on his own. And the baby's not a baby anymore (and he still has trouble with his colors. My bad).

When your children are young, you think the time is never going to pass with all the sleepless nights, the toys strewn all over the house, and the endless carpools. But then, you wake up one morning and the house is quiet. Eerily quiet. The teenage friends stopping over, the blaring music, the raids on the refrigerator are all things of the past. And if you're honest with yourself, you really do miss it.

"The boys grew up."
Genesis 25:27

CHAPTER NINE

You Talkin' to Me?

I have to be honest with you. I thought after twenty-five years in the entertainment business, I would be a has-been by now. Tami, always the voice of reason in our home, has just read that sentence over my shoulder and has informed me that in reality I am a never-was-been. Wives are good at keeping us humble, aren't they? I think it may be their calling.

But Tami might be right. My career has been steady, but not stellar. I haven't done *The Tonight Show* yet or *Letterman* or even *Conan,* for that matter. I have sat in their audiences and believe my left ear was caught on camera twice. But I have never been a featured guest.

Entertainment, unlike most other lines of work, has certain expectations that if not met could cause a lesser man self-esteem problems. Self-esteem issues aren't all that unusual in the entertainment industry. An entertainer with self-esteem problems is about as rare as a celebrity in rehab. This could be why so many entertainers feel justified in asking for such astronomical salaries. It's so they'll feel better about themselves. Let's face it, in a material world, twenty million bucks per movie buys a lot of distractions.

I am a recovering alcohol- and drug-addicted entertainer with self-esteem problems. Come to think of it, this could be why I have so many other issues. I am a walking, talking cliché! My self-esteem might have been stronger if I had been good at something else. But comedy was it. All my life, the only thing I was reasonably adept at was making people laugh. So I decided to take it to the stage and become a stand-up comic.

I was going to bring about world peace through my humor.

OK, to be perfectly honest, I really got into comedy because I liked the hours, or as my wife says, "the hour". Nothing fits a bystander's lifestyle more than working only one hour a day. As good as that schedule sounds, it had its problems. Mainly, what does a person who thinks he's a garden slug do with himself for the other twenty-three in the day? A man can bowl only so many frames, if you know what I mean.

Most of the time, I spend my free hours just lying around the house and thinking. I have no way to prove this, but maybe this is how a garden slug spends his free time too—just hanging out with the wife and kids, pondering the meaning of life, and trying his best to stay out of everyone's way.

I am often asked what I did before I became a stand-up comedian. It's a fair question. A person's identity is partly defined by the jobs he's held. Of course, my wife will tell you that her identity comes from the bat cave in which she dwells in her other life as a crime-fighter. (Sorry, Tami, I couldn't resist that, and I am not taking it out.)

Like most comics, I have a long list of former jobs. In the beginning, you often perform for free. So to eat, you need a paying job too. But because not every employer can be accommodating enough to work around your performance schedule, you end up going through a lot of hirings and firings. I believe I have held almost every job known to man for forty-eight hours or less.

The only nonentertainment job I had for any length of time was as a night manager at a minimart. That's right, I said *manager*. I was twenty and I was already master of my domain. I realize manager is a little ambitious for a bystander, but as much as I tried to hide my natural supervisory skills, the owner apparently saw through my facade and hired me on the spot to run the place.

You should have seen me at the job interview. Talk about self-assured. I was fresh out of GED class, where I had finished second behind a biker mother of six. (The only reason she did better than I was because she had more of an incentive to excel. She had seven mouths and a Harley to feed, and I'm pretty sure she was still making payments on all the tattoos.)

So, with my GED in hand and feeling like the world was my oyster, I had answered the minimart's ad for a "bright, ambitious self-starter." And I landed the job. The fact that no one else had applied and the store had been robbed four times in the previous six months was beside the point.

I was feeling pretty impressed with my supervisory title until I got to work and realized I was the only person working there. I was a manager in charge of a crew of one: me. I wasn't sure how that arrangement was going to work out because my forte as a manager and a bystander would certainly be delegating responsibility. But I gave it the ol' college . . . er, GED try.

Things were going fine until I started letting the title go to my head and coming down too hard on my crew. I would bark out orders to myself. "Who's going to stock these shelves?" I'd say.

"All right, all right," I'd say. "Just stop yelling at me!"

I know this could be considered talking to myself, which in some circles might be considered a little loony. But loony people don't get paid for being loony. And I was getting a weekly check.

But I've always talked to myself and I'm quite comfortable doing so. A lot of perfectly normal people talk to themselves. Besides, self-talk is the language of a bystander.

However, I have been noticing that the older I get, the more I have to raise my voice so I can hear me. Or maybe I'm just tuning myself out, saying to myself, "The old codger. What does he know?" Whatever the reason, my self-shouting matches are starting to draw crowds. I've tried to tell myself to consider my public image, but I won't listen to a thing I say.

Recently I caught myself having an argument with me in the middle of the canned food aisle at the Wal-Mart Supercenter. I didn't remember canned beets ever costing that much. Then, a part of me did remember, but I told that part that it wasn't beets I was referring to, but cranberries.

"Same thing," I said.

"You're telling me that cranberries and beets are the same thing?" I said.

"Don't raise your voice at me!" I said.

"I did not raise my voice!"

"Did too!"

"Did not!"

"Did too!"

"Just leave me alone. I'm the one writing this book. If you want to tell your lies, then write your own book! The truth is on my side!"

Things turned ugly after that. Suffice it to say, this self-conversing can become a problem if you're not careful. My only saving grace is that the cellular phone companies offer a cord that hangs out of your ear and a microphone that dangles by your mouth, allowing you to talk to whomever you want, whenever you want, hands-free. So now I can walk up and down the aisles of Wal-Mart, arguing with myself to my heart's content, and no one will even look twice. It's the perfect bystander's Christmas gift (if you're reading this, Tami, that hint's for you).

But to make a long story short . . .

"Who are you kidding? That's impossible."

"Is that you again?"

"Get to the point of the chapter, will you?"

"I'll get to the point when you get a clue!"

Sorry. Just ignore us. Before rehab this is why I got drunk in the morning. It was crowd control. And that's precisely why I had such a difficult time supervising myself. Things got so bad at the minimart that, as the manager, I eventually had to fire myself. It was a tough decision, but I didn't like my attitude. I was always saying negative things about the store and its customers. By itself, that might not have made a good case for the termination, but then I got the just cause I needed. I caught myself stealing. Not once, but three times over a period of three weeks. I had been taking my paychecks when I wasn't looking. Naturally, I tried to deny it, but I saw myself on video.

Firing myself was the toughest thing I've ever had to do. I even started to cry, which really disappointed me. I couldn't believe I was playing the sympathy card like that. I told myself to get out and not come back. I would be mailing my final paycheck to my house. Of course, I didn't believe me. I took myself to the labor board but I hired the best attorneys around, and how could I stand up against that kind of power?

So I left without even telling myself good-bye.

Looking back now, maybe my minimart era wasn't as bad as I remember. There were some fun times. I really enjoyed watching the customers. I worked from 11:00 P.M. to 7:00 A.M., which in the business is known as the graveyard shift. They call it that because the people buying groceries at 2:00 A.M. are usually embalmed. They've just left a myriad of bars and saloons and are pickled beyond recognition. When it comes to being personable, though, these folks shine. The ones that would stop by our store looked like a group of extras from a Stephen King project, and they all wanted to be my best friend. I didn't fall for it though. I knew they were just being nice because I was the guardian of their treasure.

"Hey, dude, where're you keeping the SpaghettiOs?" they'd grumble as they stumbled toward me. To which I would reply in similar lingo, "Hey, dude, there are only three aisles. Why don't you try to figure that out on your own? Get a sense of accomplishment for once in your life." Then I would smile, according to the minimart handbook. I always smiled. I believe it was my smile that made me Employee of the Month three times in a row.

"I deserved that. I was the harder worker."

"Are you back again? I thought we were past all that?"

"Go on, but just remember: I'm watching you."

Anyway, these late-night customers would come in, grab some SpaghettiOs or some other canned Italian delicacy, and begin their death march to the microwave oven. They were so out of it, they had no idea what they were doing. As they opened the microwave door, there were times I considered saying something about cans and microwaves, but then I would think, *No one could be so stupid as to put an aluminum can into a microwave and fire that baby up.*

You know, the depths of ignorance in this country no longer cease to amaze me. Not only would they put the can into the oven and nuke it, they would press their faces against the glass door to watch, even calling their pickled pals over to enjoy the fireworks show.

"Dude! Get a load of the sparks!"

I was sure that as the microwave vibrated and shook, somewhere in the neighborhood, maybe three or four blocks away, there was some guy with a pacemaker, clutching his chest and screaming, "Ah, honey, they're cooking another can again!"

But it wasn't the SpaghettiOs people who bothered me the most. It was the shoplifters. Now as a bystander, I am not going to lose my life over a package of Twinkies. If someone wants Twinkies that bad, he can have all he wants. I'm not going to risk my life over two oblong little sponge cakes, no matter how good their filling is. So the fact that these people were stealing didn't bother me as much as how they thought I didn't know they were stealing. I may not get involved, but I do have eyes, and I'm not stupid. I know the difference between a lazy procrastinator and an ignorant moron.

"Do not."

"You again? That's a violation of your restraining order!"

"Is not."

"Is too."

Sorry, I digress.

"It's 'we.' Get your pronouns straight, you ignorant moron. Stop procrastinating and finish your story."

Thank you.

There were people who would stuff a pack of Twinkies in their pants (and this was before the huge-pants craze of the past couple years in which kids can stick a Volkswagen in their drawers and no one would notice). Back then, the hoodlums wore their jeans tight. They would shove merchandise in their pants, then walk around pretending to shop with a big lump sticking out of their pockets. It's not going to take Columbo to piece this crime together. Especially because cellophane is not the quietest material ever produced. Strolling around the store, these guys would sound like they were walking on cornflakes.

Eventually, one of the hoodlums would say to the other, "I don't see nothin' here. I'll wait for you in the car." (Wink, wink.) Then he would start to walk toward the door.

If only for my own sense of dignity, I had to stop him and call him over to the register. I know I'm a bystander, but this was elementary, my dear Watson.

"Hey, dude, come over here," I would say.

The hardest thing at this point was keeping a straight face. As the lad would crunch his way over to the counter, I'd notice him trying to turn to an angle that would conceal the bulges in his pants.

"Yeah, whatcha want?" he'd slur.

I would reach over and push on the square bulge. Crunch. "What's this?" I would ask.

"What?"

I'd poke it again. Crunch. "That," I'd say.

Embarrassed, he would spit out some lame excuse: "My underwear?"

Not wanting to confront the guy and violate the first rule of bystanderism, I would suggest a solution to his obvious problem.

"Sounds like they need a bath," I'd say. "Perhaps you would like to buy a box of Tide. It's on aisle 3." (Being the manager means knowing how to upsale.)

Other shoplifters were a little more dramatic. They would run out of the store with their Twinkies like we were staging an episode of *COPS* or something. I never understood this kind of thinking. Why all the energy? Did they really believe I would leave my register unmanned and chase them three blocks to tackle them?

If they needed a sugar rush that bad, they had more problems than kleptomania.

Needless to say, the manager position wasn't for me, but after firing myself, I had more time to pursue the one-hour-a-day job that proved to be far better suited to me—comedian. As a comedian, I have an audience I can talk to, so I no longer have to talk to myself.

"Yeah, like they want to listen."

"I'm not talking to you. I'm talking to the reader."

"What reader?"

"You don't know how many people have bought this book."

"Your mom and who else?"

"It's on the *New York Times* best-sellers list."

"You penciled it in yourself. That doesn't count."

"Does too."

"Does not."

Pay no attention to him. You'll only encourage him.

*"Moreover, when God gives any man wealth and
possessions, and enables him to enjoy them,
to accept his lot and be happy in his work —
this is a gift of God."*
Ecclesiastes 5:19

CHAPTER TEN

Just Tell Me What You Want!

On a recent plane flight, I read an article that basically says all this talk about communication is overrated. I won't go into great detail, or any detail for that matter, on what the article actually said because my short-term memory is too short, and I couldn't really concentrate on the article anyway because of the two-year-old behind me kicking my seat. But please note: for the writer to get his point across, he had to communicate it. Am I the only one who sees the irony in that?

We're living in an age of contradictions. Especially when it comes to politics. The Democrats accuse the Republicans of the very thing they're doing at the very same time they're making the accusation. And the Republicans accuse the Democrats of hypocrisy while they're doing the very same thing they're accusing the Democrats of doing. Even third-party candidates, who love to piously point fingers at the hypocrisy of both major parties, do their own fair share of talking out of both sides of their mouth. It's as if the only person they agree with is Groucho Marx, who once said, "Those are my principles, and if you don't like them, I have others."

Is it any wonder that only about half of us vote in our elections?

But even with all the hypocrisy and contradictions in politics and life, communication is still very important. That is why I disagree with the writer of the magazine article. We have to have healthy communication with each other. It's the only way that we can . . . excuse me while I communicate with the little lad behind me.

OK, now that I have his attention, and his toes out of my rib cage, allow me to continue with my book and illustrate the point of this chapter — communication.

When I look at my parents, I think they are still married today because of their ability to communicate with each other. Not on a surface level, like you have with the person taking your order in a drive-through lane (although repeating your order six times tends to draw you a little closer together emotionally). The communication my parents enjoy is a lot deeper than that — it's the kind you could have only with a person you've lived with for more than fifty years.

I first detected my mother and father's communication skills when Tami and I were visiting them for the holidays last year. We were sitting in the family room, watching a football game, when out of nowhere my father let loose a couple of grunts, belches, and other bodily noises topped off with a sigh.

Ten minutes later my mother showed up carrying a couple of hot dogs and a soda pop for the old man. Obviously, the grunting and sighing was their own special language. As far as

I know, this language is not offered at any of the colleges and universities of our nation, although I'm pretty sure most men are already fluent in the grunting dialect.

I remember asking my wife later if she thought we would ever get to that level of communication. I was moved by the spontaneity and succinctness of her reply. "Shoot me if we do," she said. That's why I love my little bran muffin. She has always been such the romantic.

I have shared this personal story with you in hopes of springboarding us into a discussion on the different ways in which men and women, parents and children, fast-food workers and customers, politicians and voters, and the whole world (for that matter) communicate.

One of the most important aspects of communication is listening. For communication to work properly, you have to pay attention to what the other person is saying. This isn't easy because we live in a visual society. But if God didn't think listening was important, why would He have provided us with a backup plan? The Almighty gave us not one, but two ears. He didn't give our mouths a backup. It was just one to a customer, as if God were saying, "You wear that one out and you're on your own." So if you want to improve your communication with others, listen more and talk less.

Good communication in marriage also means knowing how to handle disagreements. I don't mean going to your corners and waiting for the bell to ring. I'm talking about healthy conflict resolution. In my own life, I've found that getting to a quick resolution usually means someone has to admit being wrong. That's a job that's always been on my honey-do list. Even when I'm clearly in the right, it is my job to apologize.

Excuse me while I apologize to the boy sitting behind me just to prove my point.

See, that's how good I've gotten at it. I have found that all it takes is someone to make the first move, and usually the other party will apologize for the initiator's thoughtless behavior too. The kid behind me is a perfect example. I apologized and now he . . . all right, so he's kicking the seat again. Obviously, this method may not work with two-year-olds.

In my marriage, I don't mind being the first to apologize because I have discovered that the sooner I start eating humble pie, the sooner I can get to the golf range to hit some balls. (Have you noticed humble pie is the one dessert all wives let their husbands have seconds, thirds, and fourths of?)

My wife just told me to apologize for saying that I always apologize first because she claims that she's the one who apologizes first. But apologizing (even when you're in the right) just so you don't have to waste anymore energy on the fight is a bystander trait, and we've already established that I am the bystander in the family.

She just asked me to apologize again for saying that I'm ever in the right. Because I'm on a deadline, I will do as she wishes or I'll never finish. (I'm also making a mental note to write my next book in my closet.)

When Tami and I were newlyweds, we had no idea how to communicate. I spent a lot of energy trying to get my young bride on board my train of thought. But more often than not, my train left the station without her—regardless of it being on the right track or even on a track at all—and the only thing that did was make her want to derail me. Tami didn't want to come around to my way of thinking, and I didn't want to come around to hers. So there we were, both of us more interested in protecting our pride, being right, and getting the last word. We rarely listened to each other, so our lives were filled with misunderstandings and hurt feelings.

But over the years, we've learned to communicate better and to have healthy disagreements. We know how to say exactly what we mean and make sure the other person has heard exactly what we've said. We argue less now yet get more of our own desires met. Funny how that works.

We've also learned how to get people to see our point of view: learn their way of communicating, then use that same method in our communication with them. This takes time and perhaps Prozac on occasion. All right, I'm just kidding about the Prozac. But suffice it to say, learning how to properly communicate with your spouse and others in your life is a lot of work.

It took two years of marriage for me to figure out that Tami will never directly tell me to do a chore. If she wants me to do something, she will ask a question, and from that question I am to decipher what she wants me to do. It's a little game many wives seem to enjoy playing with their husbands. This has literally kept me in a perpetual state of confusion the entire twenty years of our marriage. Call me psychic, but after twenty years, I am beginning to think this is by design. Most bystanders' home state is that of Confusion, but I do like to travel out of it once in awhile.

This is how my wife plays the game. Say I leave a pair of my underwear in the middle of the bedroom floor. I know it's difficult to imagine that someone such as I would be that insensitive, but please, just go with me on this illustration.

So there are my unmentionables, lying in the middle of the room, and that "frosts" my wife. *Frost.* That's my wife's favorite word. If someone cuts her off on the highway, she will mumble, "Oh, that just frosts me."

If I'm not "frosting" her, I am "driving her up the wall." There have been days when the kids stop me in the hall and ask, "Where's Mom?" "I believe she's up the wall with frostbite," I usually reply. "You won't believe what put her there," I continue. "It was that pair of underwear in the middle of the room." When you think about it, my drawers are the most powerful pair of underwear known to mankind. Not only can they defy gravity, but they also have the ability to alter temperature to polar lows. Amazing, isn't it, that a single pair of underwear could have that kind of power? And they are mine. I wonder what something like that could bring me on eBay?

So, yes, I confess, I have been known to leave my shorts on the floor, but I do have an explanation. The habit was set when I was single and would simply do it as a time-saver. You see, as the shorts succumbed to gravity during my walk to the shower, I could just let them slide down and eventually come to rest on the floor and step right out of them. No effort required. By keeping them in the middle of the floor, I could also easily monitor my underwear inventory. If there were four pairs on the floor, I knew there must be eight left in the drawer. This system worked flawlessly for years. Then I got married, and I found out that it "frosts" my lovely wife.

To a certain extent I can understand her frosting. I realize all too well that my wife did not come into my life to be my maid. I may have gotten that concept embroidered on our towels. And sheets. And it might even have been the salutation on a few birthday cakes, but deep down, I know it's not the case. I know that because she tells me that truth all day long.

"I am not your maid!" she says. That may be vague, but I believe the hidden meaning is, she is not my maid. I was so happy when our children were born because she finally had others to tell that she was not their maid.

I certainly don't want to generalize and say it's a woman's thing, but my mother used to say that very same thing to me as she picked up things around my room. On a typical Saturday morning at our house, my mother would walk into my room, look around, and then say in disgust, "I am not your maid!" But instead of turning around and walking out, she would start picking clothes off the floor.

"If you think I am going to . . . (pause for dramatic emphasis) . . . pick up your clothes for the rest of your life . . . (another well-timed pause) you have another think coming, young man!" she'd say with her arms full of my clothing.

This went on for eighteen years. I don't know what the other think I had coming was, but it never arrived. My point is, she would tell me she wasn't my maid, then act like she was. Whatever I left on the floor, she'd pick up. What does a teenage boy do with that? I did the only thing I knew how to do. I told her she missed a sock up on the ceiling fan.

I mention this to illustrate how saying one thing and doing another confuses people. The first time my wife told me that she wasn't my maid, I kind of smiled and said, "Oh yeah, I've heard that before."

But unlike my mother, Tami meant it. She said it the first time she found my clothes on the floor, but the second time, she kicked them at me. High in the air, right at my skull! There was no regard for my safety at all. And some of those socks had a week's worth of wear in them! In some states, I believe that's a felony. They could've easily put an eye out. But did that truth cause the slightest hesitation in my beloved wife? No. She just kicked them at me and said, "Get rid of these! I have had it!"

That's another one of my beloved's favorite sayings, "I have had it!" We all know what my wife's "had it" means at our house. It means I should check to see if bin Laden's bunker is available for a new fugitive.

Even though Tami had "had it" with my disregard for hampers, she did not understand the danger of kicking a man's dirty laundry around willy-nilly. There was one time when I couldn't get out of the way, and the shorts hit me right in the face. Any man reading this knows that if you haven't shaved, your face is like Velcro. Those boxers can adhere to you so tightly it'll take a surgical scalpel to remove them. But again, did she care? Noooo! She kicked them at me, and when I couldn't duck fast enough, they caught on my stubble and scared the living bejeebies out of me. I began running around the room, screaming, "GET THEM OFF ME! GET THEM OFF ME!" I am not touching my own underwear; that's why I learned to walk out of them in the first place.

Tami, finally feeling guilty for putting my safety in such jeopardy, ran over and peeled the shorts off my face—which made that grating Velcro sound, of course—then left me on the floor, whimpering like a wet dog. As she exited the room, I could hear her mumbling, "I've got a whole houseful of ingrates!"

"*Have*," I said. "It should be 'I *have* a whole houseful of ingrates.'"

You see, even in my pain, I was the one trying to communicate. But by that time, she was in no mood to talk.

As I lay there, analyzing our impasse and replaying everything she had been saying up to that point, the reality of the situation slowly became clear to me. What Tami had been saying, in her own sweet way, was that it was disrespectful of me to leave my stuff lying around the house. Even though it didn't bother me, it bothered her, and my actions were saying a lot more than I thought they were. In fact, my actions were screaming at her that picking up after me was all she was worth. My thoughtlessness was pricking her self-esteem. So I stopped long enough to mentally replay what she had been saying, only this time I actually listened and finally "heard" her.

Now when I walk out of my underwear on the way to the shower, I'm much more respectful. I kick them under the bed. That way she can't see them.

Not picking up after myself isn't the only thing that has caused us communication problems over the years. There have been plenty of other issues. But rather than go into detail, let me say that my life would be so much easier if Tami would verbalize what she really wants. Not the subtle hints. Not the innuendos. Not the games. Just honest-to-goodness communication. Even as I type this, though, I can hear all you women reading this and scoffing that if you were perfectly frank, we still wouldn't catch on. But I can also see all of you men, nodding your heads and saying, "Just give us a chance!"

Give us a chance—that's one of a man's few requests for the woman he loves. We don't want sweet talk. We want clear talk. Just tell us what you want! The only games we like are organized sports—football, baseball, basketball . . . that sort of thing. We're not good at word games.

In other words, when you want us to pick our clothes up, don't say, "Are those yours?" Say, "Please pick up your clothes."

When you want us to let you watch your program on television, don't say, "Why do I bother?" Say, "Can I watch my program now?"

And when you want us to take you out to dinner, don't say, "What did I do to deserve all these ingrates." Say, "I'd love to try out that new restaurant down the street. I hear their drive-through lane is really fast."

In other words, talk to us. Communicate in an honest, direct manner. Tell us what you want. It's a simple concept, but a powerful one. If couples, parents and children, and politicians and voters would start doing this, our whole world could change. Let's quit saying one thing to each other and meaning something else.

I can't tell you how many evenings I've wandered aimlessly through my living room with a coat hanger wrapped around my cranium, looking bewildered and staring up at the ceiling. My sons will stop what they're doing and ask, "Whatcha doin', Pops?" And I answer, "I'm trying to divine what your mother wants. There has to be a signal around here somewhere. Perhaps if you wrap me in aluminum foil, it will make me a better conduit."

This process uses up all the Reynolds tin wrap in the house, and come Thanksgiving, my wife is pretty frosted with me because she has nothing to wrap the bird in, but this is what I have been driven to. She doesn't see her fault in any of this. She just shakes her head and says, "Why, God? Why?"

That's another one of Tami's favorite sayings. To me that sounds more like a prayer, but I've learned that there is probably a hidden message in there for me too.

That's why I must repeat to the ladies, *please just tell us what you want!*

My favorite miscommunication story of all came after about four months of marriage. I was walking through our living room, golf clubs on my shoulder, golf shoes in hand, on my way to go golfing. Just as I was ready to walk out the door, Tami asked me a question. Any married person reading this should have a pretty good idea of the question I was asked. That's right. She said, "Where are you going?"

Now, I was a naive young husband with only a few months of marital bliss under my belt, so I said sarcastically, "I am going bowling, Columbo."

Weeeeeeeeeeell, apparently, that was the wrong answer. Two hours later I was still in my living room being grilled by Columbo. At one point, I realized there must be something else going on with her, so I asked, "What is this really about, honey?"

Weeeeeeeeeeell, she started telling me. As I was late for my tee time, I wasn't really paying attention, but I did catch some of the words. It was something like "blah, blah, blah," then "Why didn't I listen to my mother? Blah, blah, blah."

But even then I was trying for honest communication, so I said, "Look, honey, I just want you to hurry up and get to the point so I can still make the back nine."

Another wrong answer.

The "blah, blah, blahs" got a little more specific at this point. But I still couldn't see why all of this communication was taking so long.

These communication problems have continued throughout our marriage, until one night not too long ago when I finally put my foot down. I stood at the edge of our bed and said to the wife of my youth, "Baby, I will climb mountains for you. I will swim rivers for you. I would even slay a beast for you! Just quit talking in code and *tell me what you want!*"

At that point, my wife had this A. D. D. bystander's complete and undivided attention. I was ready to listen to whatever she had on her mind.

"All right," Tami said. "You want to know what I want?"

"Yes! Yes!" I said, pleading with her to at long last be completely honest with me.

"Fine!" she said.

Uh-oh. Immediately I got a sick feeling in the pit of my stomach. I could tell from the look on her face that this was a moment that she, too, had been longing for. If I've learned anything through our lives together, it's that whenever my wife says "fine" in that way, it means everything BUT fine. She has been known to use the word *fine* as a noun — a sort of club with which she pummels me over the head. My instincts are to duck and run whenever she brings out this seemingly innocent word. But I didn't run. I stayed and took it like a man . . . or at least a good bystander. I started backpedaling just a little (it's called male self-preservation). I said, "Don't worry about it, babe. It's not that important. I will somehow figure it all out like I always do. Maybe Amazon has a male-female translation book."

I started to leave the room, thankful that I had managed to get out of yet another "fine" confrontation. Anyway, it was my own fault that I hadn't understood what Tami wanted. I had forgotten to wear my aluminum foil and coat hanger. What did I expect?

But Tami wasn't going to let me off the hook that easily.

"You really want to know what I want?" she said, moving in for the kill.

"It's OK," I said, backpedaling as fast as I could. "I kind of like living in the dark. I've got sensitive eyes anyway."

"I will tell you what I want!" she said, then dove into a twenty-minute tirade on everything that had been building up over the past few months. "I want you to clean out the sink after you shave! If I wanted a fur-lined sink, I would have bought one!"

OK. Fair enough.

She continued: "I want you to put the toilet seat down! And if you don't, when I sit in the water, I would appreciate your not laughing!"

That one wasn't going to be easy, but I nodded.

"I want you to just once ask me how my day was. And when I begin to tell you, don't interrupt me and start telling me about your round of golf!"

Wait a minute. She didn't want to hear about my golf?! Now, that one hurt. But because this chapter is on honest communication, I honestly have to confess that it was the very mention of my golf game that made me start thinking about golf. Until then, Tami had my undivided attention. But that's how my brain works. The power of suggestion—it's like the plague to someone with A. D. D. My mind went to the fur-lined sink image too. When she mentions a place, my mind drifts there, and I'm powerless to stop it. I don't hear a word she's saying after that; so as you can see, most of the fault lies with her amazing gift for imagery.

I finally came back to the moment just as she was calling my name: "Jeff! Jeffrey, what are you doing?"

I wanted to confess that I was just about to hit a nine iron to six feet from the pin, hoping she'd see the humor in my mind going where she sent it, but if I've learned anything in comedy, it's timing, and this was definitely not the right time for humor. It would have been my third wrong answer, and my wife operates under the "three strikes and you're out on the sofa" rule.

Instead, I was about to say, "I was just thinking about the loveliness of you, my little sweet potato," but she was on a roll and wouldn't let me get a word in edgewise.

"Look, I could spend my days telling you what I want, but it doesn't matter because you don't listen to me anyway, do you?"

What was she talking about? I asked myself. Not as a defensive thought (as though I always listen when she speaks) but as a plea because I wasn't listening again and would soon be in big trouble. Think! Think!

I could tell from the look on her face that she had just asked me a question, but my mind had already gone back to the golf course. I knew I had been set up. By my own wife, even. It had been a trap, and I walked right into it. By asking me a question, she would see if I had been paying attention. I played it safe and opted for silence.

She waited.

I waited.

She waited some more. Finally, she looked me in eye and said, "You weren't listening, were you?"

I waited for a good answer to come to me, but none did.

"Listen, Jeff, the truth is, if I have to tell you what I want and you do it, it won't mean much to me because I had to tell you that I wanted it. But if you guess at what I want, and you get it right, that means you care."

I would have liked her to repeat that, but I already had a headache. So I took my chances and replied, "What if I guess and get it wrong?"

"That's a risk you take."

Communication can certainly be frustrating, can't it?

I guess good communication really boils down to listening, sharing, and loving. Instead of making each other read between the lines, share what you really want and need. With all the uncertainty in the world today, who needs more guessing games?

These days, I'm trying to be much more communicative with my wife. If I'm walking through my living room with golf clubs on my shoulder, and my wife stops and asks where I am going, I tell her the truth.

"I'm going to put these clubs in the car, then come right back and mow the lawn, buttercup."

You gotta admit, I'm catching on.

"Your 'yes' must be 'yes,' and your 'no' must be 'no,'
so that you won't fall under judgment."
James 5:12

CHAPTER ELEVEN

Is There Dolphin Meat in That Tuna?

A number of years ago, long before I developed a relationship with Jesus Christ, I was a regular attendee of numerous twelve-step programs around the country. It wasn't like I didn't belong there; I had my share of addictions. But I also knew there had to be an answer to the overwhelming feeling that I just didn't fit in here on earth. So I, like so many other addicted-personality types, found solace in watching television by the hour, particularly news programs and daytime talk shows. When the whole world comes into your living room and you're able to sit back with a bag of pork rinds and a diet Pepsi and judge the steady parade of dysfunctional people featured on these shows, it eliminates your need for God. You become the god of your own universe, sitting in pious judgment of all who dare to enter your presence through the little magic box. Your throne is a faux-leather recliner and your regal robe features pictures of Homer Simpson, but you are king.

With the remote control, you and you alone decide who shall live and who shall be banished to airwave oblivion. The beauty of this arrangement is the lack of any opposing opinion. This is not the place for debate. Who is allowed to speak is totally in your control. You can listen for as long as you choose, then when they start saying things you don't like (and they always do), you can either turn them off or hit the mute button. The mute button is great, isn't it? You can tell off whomever you want whenever you want for as long as you want and never get interrupted. As long as your neighbors don't complain, you can yell at the talking heads to your heart's content.

The only problem with this way of living is the fact that it is in direct conflict with the way the real God designed things. (If you're not sure who the real God is, look in a mirror. That's not Him.)

Unfortunately, I hadn't learned this little fact of life yet, so I watched television and I ranted. They say it's healthy to get things off your chest. I got everything off my chest, including a couple of hairs and a freckle.

But as healthy as venting is, I have to tell you, I was never more miserable than I was during this period of my life. But during this period of my life, I learned that God uses people to deliver His messages. Whether we believe in Him or not, He can and does speak to us to reach others on His behalf. We are, or can be, His angels of mercy.

Looking back over the last ten or fifteen years, I can see where people came and went in my life, leaving me with pieces of knowledge and glimpses of God that ultimately led me to faith in Christ. Not one person delivered all the parts that would eventually make up the whole picture of who God is, but each one's participation in my journey was absolutely necessary.

Interestingly enough, not all of God's messages were delivered by Christians. As a matter of fact, a lot of what God had to say to me was delivered by some pretty shady characters — people we wouldn't ordinarily picture as being God's messengers. But that's who they became, whether any of us realized it at the time or not.

On one particular Saturday, I was asked to speak at a twelve-step meeting. They knew I was a comedian, so they wanted me to do a little comedy for them. They had also mentioned something about my getting paid for it (words that always struck a chord in my empty checkbook), so I obliged.

I did a couple skits, then while I was waiting around to get paid, another comedian who had also done a bit, stopped by to wait with me. He sat down, told me his name, and asked how I was doing. I don't know why, but I started to tell him the truth of my condition. Some people are just easy to open up to, and he was one of them. Something about him made me tell him how miserable I was and how I couldn't put my finger on the why of my condition. I went down the checklist — beautiful wife, kids who love me, a job I love — why was I so miserable?

The comic listened, then after a brief pause asked me the oddest question: "How much news do you watch?"

I thought about my answer for a moment, then said, "I don't know. Not much. Five, six hours a day, I guess. Why?"

The man continued, "Let me tell you something I've learned about news and how it is put on the air," he said. "I was in South America a few years back. I was there on business, but I had heard that the pope was in town. Now, I'm not Catholic, but who doesn't want to see the Popemobile? So I went. Amazingly, there were over a quarter of a million people there to see the pope. At one point, all two hundred fifty thousand of us were on our knees praying. It was one of the most profoundly spiritual moments of my entire life. I won't go into details about the effect this had on me, but I will say it changed my life forever."

I wasn't sure how this guy's life-altering experience in South America would make me feel any better about my current misery, but I hadn't received my check yet and was trapped.

"That night, I walked back to my hotel room and turned on the TV to see what was on the news. It turned out that CNN was at the event that afternoon. After quickly panning over all two hundred fifty thousand of us praying in unison, the camera came to rest on the hundred or so people who were there to protest the pope's visit. There always seems to be someone who thinks the pontiff is the Antichrist, though we all know that's impossible because it's Jerry Springer." (Don't write the publisher. That was a joke.)

The people still hadn't brought our checks (not an unusual position for comedians to find themselves in), so I kept on listening.

"As clear as a bell," he said, "it came to me: the news brought in only one side of God's creation, the miserable side. From that moment on, I started viewing the news differently. I began to notice the same thing was happening on every channel. The news programs tend to show us only the negative of what this earth has to offer. If you fill your head full of all that spin and garbage day in and day out, as a child of God, you are going to feel very out of place. You're going to feel like you don't belong. God doesn't make garbage, human beings do. And the world is a lot better than what they're showing us. So I've stopped watching the news. Now, I see my world through my eyes, not the lenses of some cynical news director. As I see the good that's in the world, I see that it's not such a bad place after all. I feel like I'm a better fit. Why don't you try to stop watching the news for awhile and see if your attitude changes."

Just turn off the news? That seemed like a pretty simplistic answer to all my problems, but maybe it would be a start. I did what he suggested, and the change in my attitude was almost immediate. He was right: there is little on news shows that gives us much faith in the human race. So I took them all out of my daily diet. And guess what? I lost a lot of weight. Mainly in the shoulder area. The chip was gone, and I didn't feel so buried with the cares of the world.

From that day on, I held to my no-news diet. That is, until the 2000 election. All diets have to have their temptations, and that was a strong one. The news coverage of the 2000 election was too much to resist. Once I gave in to the temptation, I was hooked. I started watching in hotel rooms as I traveled, catching a glimpse of the coverage at airports and in electronics departments in stores. My habit kept growing and growing until, eventually, I had to order a satellite dish to get it at home. During my complete news-withdrawal period, I had canceled our cable subscription and had been clean for seven years. But with the dish I could get the election coverage in English, Spanish, Chinese, Farsi, Japanese, and I'm not sure, but I think I ran across a Pig Latin channel late one night.

What fascinated me more than anything on this election debacle was how two different newscasters who are (for the most part) educated people could view the exact same information and come up with two completely different reports. If it taught me anything, it taught me that there is a huge philosophical divide in this nation. It is a credit to our democratic system that there was no blood shed during that whole episode, although, with all that chad counting, there must've been more than a few paper cuts.

My lovely wife did not share my obsession with said election. As a matter of fact, she resented my compulsion to watch every minute of the news coverage. The problem wasn't that I was watching so much television; it was that I was watching so much television without bathing or eating. At one point she was sliding food under our bedroom door so I could get some nourishment. (Pizza worked great, but the burgers just barely exceeded the height requirement.)

"Eat!" she would say from the other side of the door. "Will you please eat something! If you die of starvation, it'll reflect badly on me."

It was my own fault that I couldn't tear myself away from the television set, but still, she was worrying unnecessarily.

"Quiet, woman," I said. "I need to know who's ahead!"

As I lay in bed on day five, minding my own, and America's, business, she walked into our bedroom and threw a wood-burning kit in my lap. She smiled and said that as long as I had resigned myself to never leave our bedroom, I might as well have a hobby.

Actually, the wood-burning kit turned out to be a lot of fun. I made a Do Not Disturb sign, which I promptly hung on our bedroom door. But I don't think she was impressed.

I won't bore you with the details or what I thought of the election outcome, but I will tell you that when the you're-wasting-your-life-away light finally came on in my head, I was watching the votes in question being shipped across the fair state of Florida. Focused as I was on the yellow Ryder rental truck, I had my epiphany. Here was this vehicle, doing maybe forty miles an hour down the freeway with a line of helicopters fol-lowing it, and I suddenly asked myself, *Why am I watching this?*

I couldn't come up with a good answer, so I stopped. Cold turkey. Just like that, I turned it off. Never to watch the news again . . . until the next big news item comes along. Then I'll probably fall off the media wagon and become a hopeless news junkie again.

The funny thing is that as a bystander, I really don't have an opinion on anything, much less anything political. I watch, but I don't lean one way or another. I get mad at everyone equally. In fact, it wasn't until the other day that I finally caught the end of a Sean Penn interview on television and asked my wife what it had been about. She told me that Sean Penn is a peace activist.

"Sean Penn?" I asked, surprised.

She nodded.

Sorry, but I couldn't help myself. "When did he stop beat-ing up photographers long enough to become a peace activist?" I asked.

I could see the disappointment on her face—that telltale look that says, *Why doesn't he keep up?* She smiled condescend-ingly, then said, "Perhaps if you stopped burning wood long enough to watch the world around you, you would know how sensitive Sean is these days."

Now, I ask you, isn't that just like a wife? She's the one who got me the wood-burning kit in the first place! But she was turning my enjoyment of her gift into a sarcastic assessment of my celebrity knowledge.

Luckily, my bystander ways have not been passed on to my middle son, Ryan. He came to me a few months back for one of those, you know, delicate discussions. Once again, I was just standing there in my kitchen minding my own business, when I heard, "Hey, Dad, can we talk?"

"Sure, son," I said, bracing for the worst. "What's on your mind?"

"Is there dolphin meat in that tuna fish sandwich?"

Dolphin meat? That's what he wanted to know about? My lunch? Not girls? Confused, I said, "I don't know. Does it matter?"

Ryan then launched into a fifteen-minute dissertation on how abused the dolphin is and how our little finned friend is a protected species. This was way too much information for me, and, besides, all I wanted was to get back to my wood-burning. I was contemplating searing "Sean Penn for President" into a plaque. But then my son told me that he'd finally figured out what his field of interest in college would be—animal rights activism.

When he said this, I almost choked on my tuna/quite-possibly-dolphin sandwich. My son, an activist? Don't get me wrong. As I explained to Ryan, it will be difficult to be an activist from the living room couch with a remote. "I believe it is the root word *active* that is going to cause you the most problems."

Still, I was intrigued by the whole tuna/dolphin controversy, so I did a little research of my own. Not just for the dolphin's sake, but for the underdog's sake—the unappreciated tuna. Maybe my son was wrong. Maybe the tuna is protected just like the dolphin, but no one cares. Maybe it's just a matter of the dolphins getting all the press.

It turns out that my son, the budding activist, was right. Dolphins are indeed a protected species, but tunas are on their own.

I told my son he was right. Parents hate admitting things like that. But then I added my own spin on the issue: "I think

I've figured out why the tuna is in the can and the dolphin isn't, son."

"Really?"

"Yeah, it's quite simple. The tuna can't entertain four thousand kids at Sea World on a Saturday afternoon. But if you can figure out a way to get a tuna to jump through a hoop, maybe we can move the poor thing up a few notches on the old food chain."

Ryan wasn't moved by my passion. I believe he wanted me to show a little more respect for Flipper. But he was reading me all wrong. I'm not anti-dolphin; I'm just pro-tuna. The way I see it, who's standing up for the chicken of the sea?

When you get right down to it, do animals really need to have rights? Hear me out. Before you sit down to write me a letter to chastise me on the matter, let me explain my theory. People can and should give animals love and respect. That's a given. But animal "rights" seem a murkier area. For one thing, if animals have rights, wouldn't we need to give them legal representation? And if so, how would that work? One day, you could be sitting at home when there's a knock at the front door. You open it and see a raccoon standing on your porch wearing a neck brace, screaming at his attorney next to him, "That's the guy! He left me on the side of the road to die!"

I can see the commercials now—four or five animals sitting around a big swimming pool, drinking mint juleps and looking into the camera, saying, "Thank you, Jacoby and Meyers."

Sure, laugh if you must, but I remember laughing when someone told me I would be paying eighty bucks a month to watch television. I also remember a day when I scoffed at the idea of spending my hard-earned money for drinking water.

Maybe my comedian friend was right. Maybe life would be better if we all turned off our television sets and didn't get involved. That's the bystander way, after all. Live and let live. The world doesn't need our opinions. Too many people are sharing theirs already. Sure, there are problems to solve, but if we can't solve them all, why solve any of them? The earth will keep on spinning whether it hears our two cents' worth or not. The sun will continue to rise and set whether the stock market is up or down. Why should we stress over trying to make this world a better place? Why should we care about who wins our elections? Why should we keep our oceans clean or plant a tree? Why should we do anything to save a few of God's creatures from extinction? It's too much work. Let tomorrow take care of itself. Nobody else cares, so why should we?

And besides, there are all the little wooden signs I still need to burn.

"The Lord knows man's thoughts;
they are meaningless."
Psalm 94:11

CHAPTER TWELVE

At Least You Have Your Health

———

"AAAAAAAAAAAAAAHHHHHHHHHHHHHHH!"

The scream pierced the air. Outside, I immediately dropped the wedge in my hands and bolted toward my wife's cry, passing Ryan on the way into the house.

"What was that?" he asked, worried.

I said, "It's Mom. She may be in trouble!"

Tami shows dogs for a living, and on occasion, a client's dog has gotten loose and attacked her. I assumed this was one of those times. Passing through the front door, Ryan and I heard Tami let out another cry, "Jeeeeeeeefffffff! Hurry!"

Panic-stricken, I increased my pace. The adrenaline in my veins was pumping full speed. Ryan and I arrived at the bedroom door about the same time. We quickly scanned the room for the source of her panic, but all we saw was Tami standing in the middle of the room, holding what appeared to be the remnants of a dress. She glared in my direction.

"How could you?" she asked, trying her best to recapture some composure. Ryan looked at me, at the garment, at me again, then sheepishly walked out of the room. He had a strong hunch that his mother and father were going to be having another one of their "discussions," and he was sure he had homework to do.

I longed to go with him, but something told me I'd better stay. Actually, Tami was that special something as she said, "Don't you even think about leaving, Jeff!"

Truthfully, my wife and I have had so many of these discussions over the years that all of the acrimony has dissipated. We don't ever really say anything during these moments because it is understood by both parties that I am the one who messed up. I've been guilty 99.99999 percent of the time, so it's just a given. Long ago, Tami surrendered any hope of trying to change me or raising her expectations of me, but that still doesn't stop her from feeling the frustration that comes with discovering yet another bug in the Jeff Operating System.

Before I explain what my latest malfunction was, I think it would help if I provided a little background. It's no secret to those who know me that I am a hypochondriac. My MedicAlert chain is connected to every ambulance service in the state of Tennessee, with a backup connection to several in Kentucky. And unlike normal people who actually need to come in contact with a germ to catch a disease, all I have to do is read about the rare ailment in a magazine or hear it covered on the evening news, and I start feeling all of the symptoms. I once diagnosed myself with lupus after overhearing a conversation at a Cracker Barrel. My tests came back negative. The doctor told me that my "reddish brown nodules" were nothing more than zits. But I am still keeping an eye on them. Doctors have made mistakes. Who knows how many people are setting off airline security alarms because they have scalpels bouncing around inside of them from a forgetful surgeon? Maybe lawyers need to tattoo warning labels on our abdomens that say Not to Be Used as a Medical Bag.

I do find a certain sense of irony in my hypochondria, especially because during my days in the throes of alcoholism and drug addiction, I never gave my health much of a thought. I used to say that I wasn't sick very often because no self-respecting germ would house itself in my derelict body.

But now that I've been sober for nearly twenty years, I have, for some reason or another, become obsessed with my health. Don't get me wrong; I'm still a bona fide bystander who doesn't exercise, take vitamins, or eat properly. But I am careful about germs and bacteria. And I refuse to let my hypochondria stop me. Last summer when I was bitten by a mosquito in my backyard and could feel my temperature soaring to a perilous 99 degrees, I didn't let certain malaria keep me from finishing the rest of the yard work. Absolutely not! I forged ahead and mowed my way back to health. When I cut myself on a plastic trash-bag tie and lost two pints of blood—or several drops, I'm not sure which (the dizziness overcame me)—that didn't keep me from fulfilling my "man's job" (Tami's words, not mine) of taking out the trash. So as you can see, I am a fully functioning hypochondriac.

One condition that I do have (as mentioned earlier) is Attention Deficit Disorder. But in an odd sort of way, my A. D. D. actually helps keep my hypochondria manageable. Or at least it prevents me from running up huge medical bills. You see, if my disease du jour ever gets so serious that I feel the need for immediate medical aid, I can count on my A. D. D. to distract me before I ever reach the telephone to call an ambulance. Ambulance fees can get pretty pricey for a hypochondriac. Most of them don't offer monthly passes. I've tried to lower my bills by offering to ride up front with the medic, but rules are rules, I guess.

My wife, of course, is just as skeptical of my A. D. D. as she was of my lupus, which makes me skeptical of how much attention she actually pays to me and my life.

If you think I don't have A. D. D., allow me to describe what's happened for the last hour or so of my life.

I was on my way to the computer in my bedroom to jot down some thoughts for this chapter on A. D. D., but I didn't get there because I remembered that I wanted to clean my golf clubs. After I cleaned them, I felt the overwhelming urge to dirty them again, so I thought I would hit some balls in the yard for about ten minutes.

As I started to head outside, I remembered that I had to call my manager, Lenny. Apparently this was for no reason whatsoever, as he reminded me for the fifteenth time that these things could be handled via e-mail. He was right, of course, and I could have easily done that because I was on my way to my computer. But when I put the telephone receiver down, I noticed that my putter was leaning against the wall. I thought about how nice it would be to hit a few putts. But while looking under the foot of my bed for some golf balls, I discovered an airline ticket receipt. It was the one my manager had been asking me about. I hadn't turned it in yet, and because I have to do that to get reimbursed, it was like finding cash. *Cool,* I said to myself as I picked up the telephone to call Lenny again and share my good news.

Unfortunately, he was not as thrilled as I was over my newly discovered treasure and reminded me, now for the sixteenth time, that the matter didn't warrant a phone call.

"Can't you just drop it in the mail?" he asked, as if talking to a small child. I told him he was right and that I could do that, and then I took off to find an envelope.

On my way out of the bedroom I saw my Medicus, which is a training driver used in golf to help a player's tempo (I tend to swing too fast). So I grabbed the Medicus and started to practice my swing.

After a couple of swings, I remembered my computer and my previous mission to jot down some thoughts about my A. D. D. Thus far, not a word had been jotted. So I walked back to my desk. Before I could sit down, I remembered the envelope I was supposed to get, only by now I had forgotten why I was getting it.

I stood thinking in the room for a few moments. But instead of thinking about why I needed an envelope or what I was going to write in this chapter about Attention Deficit Disorder, I started thinking about how much I could sure use a sandwich. *No wonder I can't remember anything,* I said to myself. *I'm starving!*

While on my way to the kitchen, Ryan stopped me in the hallway and asked the one question that I've repeatedly told him never to ask me: "Whatcha doin'?" I hate that question. My wife and I have had our worst fights over that question. I never know how to answer it because, to be perfectly honest, I am never *doing* anything; I always seem to be *thinking* about doing something but never really doing it.

Suspicious, I asked my son if his mother had sent him to ask me that. He said no, then pitter-pattered down the hallway.

I asked him where he was going because I know he hates that question almost as much as I hate "Whatcha doin'?"

He mumbled, "Nowhere," and kept moving.

"Well, mail me a postcard when you get there," I said.

Now, I think that's funny, so I laughed, and the laughter once again jogged my memory about jotting down some funny thoughts on Attention Deficit Disorder.

I started to walk back to the bedroom to finish working on this chapter, but then I realized I was cold. Being cold is not unusual for me. I'm always cold. It could be due to poor circulation, but I think it's more likely due to the fact that my wife, who started menopause about a year and a half ago, keeps our thermostat set at a comfortable zero degrees. And she still spends half her week screaming at the air-conditioning guy, telling him that our unit's broken. Broken? If it's broken, why are there penguins in our living room? Why do we have meat hanging from our curtain rods? Why? I'll tell you why. It's because the air conditioner is NOT broken. It's just that there is not enough Freon in the world to cool off the furnace that burns inside my bride. I have my doubts about a hole in the ozone cooling the earth's temperature, but if there is one, I would venture to guess that it's directly over the roof of my house.

Don't get me wrong: I understand my wife's need to keep the house at an arctic temperature. Menopause does that to women. So I don't fault her for something she has no control over. A good husband adjusts. I'll just start dressing a little warmer around the house. I do have a flak jacket that I got from the army surplus store. Anyway, what's a little frostbite for the woman you love? It'll add a little color to my legs. All of that is a small price to pay for buttercup's happiness.

So it's not that I begrudge her the control of the thermostat. It's just that there's a safety issue here. A few years ago my wife insisted on having a sprinkling system installed in our house, and therein lies my real issue. If our house ever did catch fire and those sprinklers engaged, the water would turn to snow before it ever hit the floor. Snow doesn't put out a lot of fires. It might eventually, but not before you've started construction on your new house.

On this particular day, though, my wife was away at the grocery store, so I had total freedom and temperature control. There I was, all set to set the thermostat to my liking, when I caught another glimpse of the airline receipt under the bed and remembered I never did take care of that. This time, I grabbed the receipt and went directly to the kitchen to find an envelope. Just as I stepped into the kitchen, my wife returned home with some groceries and asked, "Whatcha doin'?"

Aha! I said to myself because for once I was ready for the question. This time, this bystander husband was actually in the middle of *doing* something.

"Getting an envelope," I said smugly.

"Why?" she grilled.

Again, I was ready. "To mail this receipt to Lenny, so I can get reimbursed." With each question, I was gaining more confidence.

"Reimbursed for what?" she said.

I reminded my wife that I had paid for my airline ticket and was due to get reimbursed but hadn't yet because I couldn't find the receipt.

"I know that," she said. "I just want to know why you're mailing it to Lenny when you can fax it to him. That would be a lot quicker."

She was right, of course. I hadn't thought about faxing it. But I wasn't going to let her know that she was right (that kind of information is classified and must be closely guarded at all times), so I began to backpedal. Backpedaling is the bystander's favorite way to travel. I explained to Tami that it is far less stressful to simply stick the receipt in an envelope, place it in our mailbox, and let a responsible and trusted postal worker carry it across town to Lenny's mailbox than it is to shove a small receipt into a fax machine and watch it accordion-fold itself into oblivion. Even with all my logic, I could feel my edge in this discussion slowly disappearing.

Tami vehemently disagreed about mailing the receipt. Apparently, the price of a stamp was the exact amount that was going to break our budget, and she insisted that I give up my "wasteful" ways and fax the receipt.

I told Tami that I would do as she suggested, even though I knew I was going to mail it, so that at least in my own mind I could be the victor. But before I put the receipt into the fax machine, Tami interrupted again.

"Before you do that," she said, "could you get the groceries out of the car?"

I had things to do, but I couldn't think of any that sounded important enough to save me, so I walked out to the car and opened the trunk. When I lifted the bags into my arms, I spotted something shiny under some clothes that Tami had set aside for Goodwill. I moved the clothes and found my lob wedge—the lob wedge I thought I'd left on a golf course two weeks earlier. I pulled it out and was about to ask Tami why it was in a pile of clothes to give to Goodwill when I spotted some golf balls in the trunk and thought perhaps I should hit a couple of them with the wedge.

I put down the groceries and walked out to the middle of the yard and was just about to hit my first ball when I spotted yet another shiny object. I was seeing so many shiny objects, I made a mental note to get tested for cataracts.

I walked over to the glistening metal object in the grass and discovered that it was my hammer. Like most dads, I have told my kids a thousand times to put my tools back after using them. *Why can't they ever stay on task?* I wonder to myself. Then I picked up the hammer and walked back into the house.

"Where are the groceries?" Tami asked.

"Never mind those," I said. "I found my lob wedge in your trunk."

"What's a lob wedge?" she asked.

"Lob, but that is not the issue," I said. "I asked you two weeks ago if you had seen my wedge and you said no."

"Did not."

"Did too."

"Did not."

"Did too."

Here we go again. *Where do those kids get that?*

I have learned over the years that a mature exchange like this can go on forever. So as scintillating as it was, I decided to cut it short and ask my wife if she remembered what I was doing before all of this. (Don't you hate it when you realize you need the help of the very person you're upset with?) Tami reminded me that I was working on this book. And that's when it all came back to me.

I was on my way to my computer to jot down some thoughts about my A. D. D. and how it helps with my hypochondria. As I headed back to our bedroom, I recalled the hammer that I'd found. I knew I had to put it back in the garage; otherwise Tami would shove it in the drawer out on the porch (the drawer of no return). You probably have a drawer like this. No household tool ever wants to end up in there because, once inside, a tool might not escape for decades. I've been known to buy seven hammers before I remember to see how many forgotten hammers are in that drawer awaiting their rescue.

But as I walked to the garage to drop off the hammer in its proper place, I glanced down at the headline of the evening paper sitting in the driveway: "Six More Cases of West Nile Virus Cited."

West Nile? I quickly scanned the article for the list of symptoms. My heart sank when I realized I had them all! So that's why I've been having all those muscle aches and cramping. That's the cause of my soaring 99-degree temperature. It had to have been that or Lou Gehrig's disease (I had just seen a movie about that). No, actually, the more I thought about it, the more that strange scratch on my arm I had noticed earlier that morning was looking like the work of a brown recluse spider. There weren't any fang marks, and my skin wasn't discolored or anything, and no swelling, and well, it sort of looked like a pimple too, but I decided to be on the safe side and call my doctor to see if he could meet me at the emergency room STAT.

I reached for my cell phone because I can call my doctor only from my cell. You see, it doesn't matter that my kids and their friends use our home phone to call whomever they please. If I pick up the line, Tami will ask me what I am doing. If I tell her I'm calling the doctor, she will roll her eyes and tell me to hang up. It's a jealousy thing, I'm sure. Tami doesn't have the ability to self-diagnose diseases like I do, so she makes up for it by scoffing at me. She inevitably brought up the incident when I insisted she take me to the emergency room because by then I was sure I was having a heart attack. I wanted her to drive me because it would save an ambulance bill, and I figured we could also stop by Starbucks on the way.

Tami dropped me off at the hospital with my mocha frappuccino in hand, then went shopping at T. J. Maxx, no doubt to get her mind off worrying about me. Luckily, it wasn't a heart attack after all, but a torn muscle from swinging too hard with a nine iron.

So to avoid being reminded of that night for the thousandth time, I used my cell phone. While I'm dialing, though, Ryan walked by and asked, "What disease are you trying to keep from Mom this time?" Now, sarcasm at a time like this would usually upset me, but I had too much on my mind to dwell on it.

I dialed my doctor's number from memory, but for some reason, Lenny picked up the phone. I asked him what he was doing at my doctor's office, and he told me he was in his own office and that I had obviously misdialed. He then asked about my receipt, and I told him that I couldn't think about that now but would appreciate any information he had on the brown recluse spider. He, of course, offered no sympathy at all, then repeated that I should have e-mailed him instead and reminded me not to forget to mail the receipt.

I hung up and started to make my way back into the house, when I noticed my golf clubs again. So I grabbed a few balls and walked out to hit some wedges in the yard (the spider had already injected its poison into my system, so what's a few more minutes?). And that's when I heard, "AAAAAAAAAAAAAAHHHHHHHHHHHHHHH!"

That brings us back to Tami, standing in front of me, holding the remnants of her dress. I realize it was a long journey to get here, but I believe I have convinced you that I do indeed have A. D. D.

"Jeff, what was the last thing I told you to do before I left?" Tami asked. It was a rhetorical question. Tami knew that I knew what she had asked me to do. She was just trying to emphasize her point. Before I could even answer, though, she tossed the remains of her black dress at me—the dress she had asked me to take to the cleaners, the dress she had planned to wear to her banquet next week, the one about which I had promised, "No problem, babe, I'll take care of it."

"It never changes with you, does it, Jeff?" she said as she disappeared down the hall. I stood there feeling like a slug, realizing that this was just one more thing in a long list of promises I had not followed through with. One black dress not making it to the cleaners doesn't sound like much; it's just one small broken promise. And had our dogs not gotten up on the bed and shredded the dress, I'm sure Tami wouldn't have been nearly so mad at me. But while one dress may be a small thing, in the course of twenty years, all these little things add up. All the things that I had blown off with "What are you so upset about?" had a way of stacking themselves on top of each other year after year after year, and now the bill was due.

I called out to her and tried to explain that I don't do these things on purpose. I didn't say to myself, "Take her dress to the cleaners? Naw, I think I'll just let the dogs make a chew stick out of it. That'll really tick her off."

I'm not sure she even hears my apologies anymore. Or my excuses. But the truth is, I have no excuse. It is disrespectful not to do these little things for someone you love. How difficult would it have been to drop off her dress at the cleaners?

I made a mental note to be more diligent in honoring my wife and her requests.

But instead of filing it with the two thousand other mental notes I have made over the past twenty years, I actually wrote this one down and hung it on the refrigerator. I also put a note in my golf bag and one in my car. Doing nice things for my wife is too important to relegate to the back of my mind where I've filed so many other good ideas over the years. It's too easy to overlook there. Every time I drop in another mental note, I can hear an audible kerplunk inside my skull when it lands in that huge empty dark part of my brain, never to be heard from again.

This time I wanted to remember how important my wife is to me.

As I made my way toward my wife to say once again that I was sorry, I heard the car backing out of the driveway.

"Where's Mom going?" I asked Ryan, who had now reappeared because the coast seemed clear.

"To buy another dress," he said.

Then I remembered the groceries that I never got out of the trunk of her car: milk, eggs, and ice cream. She probably wouldn't be home for hours. I wondered if she'd notice them. I wondered if she'd find another dress she liked. I wondered if she'd finally admit that of all the diseases I've ever thought I've had, A. D. D. isn't that much of a stretch. And I wondered how many balls I could hit in the backyard before she got back.

And so the cycle continues.

"But when [Jesus] heard this, He said, 'Those who are well don't need a doctor, but the sick do.'"
Matthew 9:28

CHAPTER THIRTEEN

Grape-Napping Is a Crime!

The other day I was sitting around the house, picking grapes off their stems and throwing them into a colander. Not something I normally do for entertainment, but I had my reasons.

First of all, let me say that no one enjoys red grapes more than I do. It is possible to enjoy red grapes as much as I do but not more. (If you happen to disagree with me on that last statement and are up for a round of dueling grapes, feel free to e-mail my manager.)

Actually, I merely suggest you contact him because I have made it a policy not to personally respond to threatening e-mail, or in this case, grape-mail. Besides, everyone knows a reigning grape champ doesn't have to accept a duel if he doesn't want to.

Before I get to why any of this matters, let me back up a decade or so, when my son, Aaron, and I had a discussion. It was one of those father-son talks about acceptable versus unacceptable behavior, focusing on why he should leave a few crumbs in the refrigerator for the rest of the family.

One thing I keep telling my children is there is nothing they have done or are thinking about doing that I haven't done or thought about doing myself. In other words, you can't con a con man. I know them better than they know themselves. I also know the true nature of man because, contrary to the notes my fourth-grade teacher would send home to my parents, I happen to be part of the human race. And because it is from this stock that my children were born, I know that they'll have some behavioral issues. It is, as they say, a given. This is why I have never had any interest in going to the zoo. For me, it's more fun watching the human jungle in my living room with feral creatures fighting over the remote control every Saturday morning.

I realize all of this unacceptable behavior is merely payback for what I did to my parents when I was young. I also realize that my only shot at revenge will be when each of my sons has a gaggle of kids that behaves the same way they do. (I can sense your agreement on this issue as you consider your own children.) Children do keep us on our toes . . . and our knees . . . and on therapy couches, especially during the teen years.

Ah, the teen years. If revenge is truly God's, as the Bible says, then I truly believe that teenagers are the Almighty's revenge on mankind. It is as if God Himself said, "Let's see how they like it—creating someone in their own image who denies their very existence. And while we're at it, let's watch their faces when their children complain that their rules are archaic and cramping their style."

So God created teenagers. And I believe He must have giggled just a little.

And because we're on the subject of teenagers, do you know that nowhere in the Bible does it mention how old Satan was when he rejected God's authority? Personally, I believe he was around fifteen.

Now, teenagers, like the rest of us, are creatures of habit. If observed long enough, they can be quite predictable. Still, every now and then, they do something so completely beyond reason that even the most observant parent couldn't have seen it coming. Need an anecdote to illustrate my point? You're in luck.

It was just another quiet morning. As usual, I was lying in bed, minding my own bystander business, when the theft took place. And believe me, it was not going to be an easy case to solve. Here's how the clues came together.

Most children wake up hungry. So do adults, but we have a little more self-control. We can at least wait until we brush our teeth and make our way to the kitchen before stuffing our faces.

Children don't have this kind of willpower. That's probably one of the reasons why they don't brush crumbs out of their beds. They like having their snacks within reach. When they wake up in the morning, they're like prisoners of war—starving and demanding to see the person in charge.

In some ways, it's understandable. The more their bodies grow, the more food they need to sustain their high energy levels. If you don't believe me, you're probably not keeping track of your grocery bills. Either that or you're sending your kids to your neighbors' houses to eat every night (which, come to think of it, might be just the budget cut we need to buy a new car this year). Excuse me while I make a mental note of that. Kerplunk!

Generally speaking, most of us conscientious parents absorb the expense of feeding our own kids. They're our kids; therefore, they're our responsibility. By doing that, we're not only carrying our own weight, but we're also in a position to notice when the grocery bill begins to increase or decrease.

At our house, the grocery bill moves in only one direction. My wife and I have had to face the fact that those cute little garbage disposals we created are quite literally eating us out of house and home. I blame a lot of it on television ads. The way I figure it, commercials are costing my family between five and six dollars a pop. It's the power of suggestion. Pavlov's dog, etc. . . . you know. As soon as a commercial comes on the tube, the kids will scamper to the refrigerator saying the same thing: "Man, I am starving!" It doesn't matter what the commercial is about—it can be for boil ointment, and the kids will say, "Man, I am starving!"

I told my wife we could probably save money by just building a trough in the kitchen and filling it up with macaroni and cheese. It's not the greatest diet, but every day or two, we could toss a couple of hot dogs in there for protein. *(Does anyone reading this honestly believe that his or her children would mind eating out of a trough?)*

This whole "I'm starving" routine drives me nuts. This is why I believe every teenager should go on a mission trip, if for no other reason than to see that other people actually manage to survive without six meals a day.

Of course, there is no sense in debating with these kids about their state of hunger, let alone starvation, because they're making their third trip to the refrigerator in the last hour. If they just scraped the stuff that was stuck to their faces back into their mouths, they would be full for the rest of the night.

As of this writing, the oldest has a girlfriend, so I'm assuming for him this food-on-the-face thing will be passing soon. Girls seem to have that effect on boys. I know it wasn't until I started dating their mother that deodorant became important to me.

I know a lot of you are probably thinking, *Why don't you just wipe their faces?* Well, we tried that, but the only thing powerful enough to liquefy the dried food particles was my wife's saliva, and they weren't too keen on that idea. The concept may work in the animal kingdom, but human kids hate having their faces washed with their mother's spit. Still, it is powerful stuff. That could be why men are inherently more prone to spitting on the sidewalk than women. The Creator made a man's spit to be pretty harmless, but a woman's spit can take the paint off a tractor-trailer. It might even be able to eat through concrete. And it can certainly get dried macaroni and cheese off a child's face.

It didn't take the kids long to figure out what my wife was going to do when she spit into a napkin. All she had to do was start to walk across the room with it, and you could almost hear the theme from *Jaws* following her, synchronized to her every move. Then she would raise the napkin in their direction, and they would take off running, screaming like the disposable extras in a Stephen King movie. Within five seconds our living room would be turned into a rodeo. I'd have to rope 'em and hog-tie 'em while their mother went in and branded—or, rather, unbranded—their faces.

This is why kids and food need to be closely supervised. It's to save them from a greater agony.

An increase in your grocery bill might also mean that there is some thievery going on. When the boys were really little, they used to love sneaking out of bed in the morning, going into the kitchen, and doing unspeakable things with the four food groups. Then they would try to lie their way out of it.

Standing there with chocolate brownie all over their faces, they would innocently stare as I asked them, "Were you guys eating brownies?"

They would shake their heads in unison. That's lying in stereo. So I said, "I want you to go into the bathroom, look in the mirror, then come back, and I will ask you again if you were eating brownies.

I naively thought they would walk to the bathroom, see the evidence on their guilty mugs, realize they had been caught red-handed (and chocolate-faced), come back, and 'fess up. Yes, I truly did believe that, and don't think for a minute that I can't hear you experienced parents laughing out loud right now! But parenting is a process, and I still had a lot to learn—mainly that trying to reason with young children is a lesson in futility.

When my sons returned from the restroom, I noticed something different about them. Oh yeah, the brownie on their faces had been removed. Apparently, these little angels had noticed the evidence on their faces and simply wiped it off.

"Did you wipe the brownie off your faces?" I asked.

I knew they were going to continue to lie. After all, the evidence was gone. Lying would be easier. But I pressed on with my interrogation. Not because I enjoyed cornering them. OK, yes, I did enjoy cornering them, but I also wanted to watch them stumble their way through their fact-free defense, so that if they ever got better at lying, I would know what they'd look like while doing it.

I repeated my question. "Did you wipe the brownie off your faces?"

"Brownie?" they asked, almost angelically.

"Yeah, the brownie you said you didn't have for breakfast, the one that was covering your faces before you went into the bathroom and wiped it onto your mother's good towel."

I added that if they had wiped it on their mother's good towel, she was going to have to severely punish them. She wouldn't want to. But as all mothers know, white towels come with their own handbook of disciplinary action. It's the law of the land and she would have no choice.

I could see the sweat forming on their little foreheads.

They were still trembling as I walked into the bathroom and picked up the towel in question, the one that was now buried in the hamper. Sure enough, there were big gobs of fudge-y goo on it.

I returned to the perpetrators and asked again, "Did you or did you not have a brownie for breakfast?"

You probably know what happened next. What was once a unified, impenetrable front began to unravel before my eyes. I'm not talking about a little crack, but a huge gaping hole that opened up as the oldest screamed out, "It was Ryan! He cut them up. I HAD TO EAT ONE!"

Ryan, who was about six at the time, looked at me and said, "Naw-aw. It was Aaron who cut 'em! Then he made me eat it!"

"Did not!"

"Did too." (Are you beginning to sense a pattern with my life?)

I told them that all their excuses were irrelevant at that moment because the scream we were hearing was their mom, apparently just noticing the white towel. The scream actually woke our neighbor—a policeman—who came rushing over with his gun drawn, demanding to know what was going on. Tami stuck the towel in his face and said, "Look what the ingrates did to my good towels!" She demanded to know the section of the penal code that covered this misdemeanor. He holstered his gun and agreed with her that there was an ordinance against this sort of towel abuse. But he felt that jail would probably not be the answer. He said that the punishment should always fit the crime, then suggested that we keep this out of the court system and just punish the boys at home.

So we did. The towel had to be washed, the boys had to clean the mess they made in the kitchen, and they each had to admit to lying and vow to do their best to not repeat the behavior.

The point of this story is that children can sometimes tell fibs. With practice, some have gotten pretty good at it, but not to the point of fooling most parents. A similar scenario plays out between our heavenly Father and us—He doesn't have much trouble seeing through all our tales and excuses either. That and the fact that He's all-knowing should make us want to be real with Him, don't you think?

It's interesting to note the kinds of things children lie about. With our kids, it was usually about food. Like the brownies, some food item would wind up missing, and then Tami and I would have to go through the ritual of trying to figure out who wasn't 'fessing up. It would have been so much simpler if one of them would've merely confessed.

I would tell my kids that I could understand their lying to us if we were unreasonable in their punishment. But we weren't. Lying was a character issue that we couldn't ignore—like stealing. Not that my kids steal. I would categorize their taking my last ice cream sandwich as rude, yes; stealing, no.

So what does any of this have to do with red grapes?

For those who have forgotten all about the grapes, let me refresh your memory. I had been picking grapes off their stems and putting them in a colander. When I was done, I rinsed them and put them in the refrigerator to make them not only cold but also crisp. There's nothing better than biting into a red grape that crunches.

Knowing the three pounds of grapes were in the safety of the fridge, I headed out to hit golf balls at the driving range. It was about 95 degrees that day with 90 percent humidity. After hitting my usual three hundred balls in about thirty minutes, I was tired. I was exhausted not only from swinging but also from trying to explain to the range manager that all the turf I dug up will grow back in a decade or two and that he should quit his whining. (Does Tiger have to put up with this abuse? I don't think so.) The good news was that he gave me a bunch of coupons for free-range balls at his competitors' businesses. I accepted the coupons and his apology (OK, he didn't say it, but I knew in his heart he was sorry) and left for home.

As I drove home, I spotted a minimart and figured I'd stop in for a drink. But then I remembered the juicy red grapes awaiting me at home.

Now, I have always contended that misery in life mainly happens when expectations collide with reality. That being the case, I was soon to discover that I was in for another bout with misery.

I pulled into my driveway, got out of my car, and ran into the kitchen. Upon opening the refrigerator, it wasn't what I saw that shocked me; it was what I didn't see. Neither the colander nor my red grapes were there. I let out a scream, and our neighbor showed up again with his gun drawn (does this guy ever work?).

Just as we began to fill out a police report for the missing orbs of juice, in walked Aaron, my oldest, holding the colander. And yes — it was empty! Except for one lone grape.

He was about to pop that last grape into his mouth when I cracked. I don't know what came over me, but I reached for the neighbor's gun. But our neighbor, sensing my desperation, had already holstered it. I would've never tried to grab the gun from my neighbor, but I did need something to drive home my point to my son. So I grabbed a pen instead and pointed it at my son. "Put down the grape and move away from the colander slowly!" I said.

My son couldn't even begin to lie his way out of this one. I had caught him red-handed. "Tell me you didn't eat three pounds of grapes!" I said.

"I don't know," he said. "I just ate what was in the bowl."

I started to go into the difference between a bowl and a colander, but like all the other times when I have tried to educate my children over details like this, his eyes started to roll into the back of his head.

But I wasn't about to give up my position of superiority. "Boy," I said, "should we just get you a trough or put you out in a pasture, so you can graze until you explode?" (You see, I really do think the trough idea is a good one.) But he just looked at me. Like an attorney right out of *L. A. Law*, I pressed on without missing a beat.

"I can't believe you ate three pounds of grapes!"

"Is that a lot?" he asked, strangely proud of his accomplishment. And all of a sudden, so was I. In that one moment, my anger melted into a sort of shared pride with my son. The grape consumption seemed to verify his manhood. It was like he was saying, "I have eaten the grapes. Bless me now, Father."

But then I snapped back to my senses. Those were MY grapes, and I wasn't about to give him a blessing. There would be other days for blessings. Right then, I knew if I told him that three pounds of grapes was a lot, he would brag to all his adolescent little chums about what he had managed to consume and would be a hero in their eyes. I couldn't let that happen.

He had rudely taken what was not his. He had de-graped me, and you don't do that to the reigning red-grape champion.

So instead I said, "I don't know if three pounds is a lot or not, but if I were you, I'd grab a couple of magazines and try not to stray too far from the bathroom." Then I added, with a slight smirk I couldn't erase, "I will have my revenge, boy!"

"What?" he asked through his red-grape lips. "What d'ya mean?"

With as much love as I could convey at the moment, I looked my son in the eye and said, "The laughter you hear in the hallway will be mine. See you in about an hour."

In hindsight, just watching him sprint down the hallway later that day and slam the bathroom door shut was worth more than all the pleasure those grapes ever would have brought me. Maybe this is why God has reserved the idea of revenge for Himself. Sometimes a thief, even a grape-napper, getting his just desserts can really be quite satisfying.

"Surely You desire integrity in the inner self,
and You teach me wisdom deep within."
Psalm 51:6

CHAPTER FOURTEEN

I Need One of Those

Whew, I'm glad that's finally over! I've just finished watching a comedian on a late-night comedy show make fun of televangelists. That sort of thing always makes me uncomfortable. Not that I didn't agree with some of what the comic said. His act wouldn't have been funny if there weren't some truth to it, and there are a few televangelists who come across as having more passion for profit than preaching—certainly not all of them, but a few. I figure that when Judgment Day comes Jesus will sort out the sincere ones from the goats, but in the meantime I make my own judgment calls by simply turning the channel. After all, it's not my place to tell someone that he's going about his calling in the wrong way. That's for each of us to figure out on our own.

However, I do have a couple questions I would like to direct at one or two of the faith healers I've seen on the tube. Don't get me wrong—it's not that I don't trust their gift, their faith, or even their sincerity. I also believe in modern-day miracles. But I've read about the healings in the Bible, and from what I can tell, Jesus wasn't self-serving in the least. He'd say, "Get up and walk; your faith has healed you," and they'd get up and walk—simple as that. He didn't follow the healing with "Now, send Me whatever amount you can." In fact, often His follow-up was merely, "Don't tell anyone about this yet, please."

But because none of us is Jesus, and everyone's entitled to his or her own personality and style, I don't really stress over the handful of hard-sell television preachers. I just look at them the same way I look at infomercial hosts—they may whole-heartedly believe in what they're doing, but it's still a high-pressure sales pitch. Which brings me to the real point of this chapter—infomercials.

I watch infomercials, but true to my bystander ways, I don't really get involved with them. I don't write down the telephone numbers or figure out if my credit card can handle the three easy payments of only $34.99 each. I enjoy watching infomercials only for the laughs.

Late last night, however, as my wife and I were flipping through the infomercials, something happened. I noticed instead of laughing and saying, "What moron would be so stupid as to purchase that pile of landfill," my wife and I were actually considering buying a few items. When I mentioned this to my parents, they told me not to worry. They said we were just going through "the change." It's not a midlife crisis or menopause; the change I am referring to is the one my father warned my wife and I about more than a decade ago. You see, for years Tami and I sat on our we're-too-smart-for-such-hype thrones, looking down our noses at any and all who would be so gullible as to "pick up that phone and dial." We laughed at all those "if you call within the next ten minutes" sales pitches and didn't care if they made it a two-for-one special or threw in a host of other free products. We weren't biting the bait. We prided ourselves in being too savvy to be sucked into that cavern of useless products.

But for some reason that night, the infomercial world suddenly had appeal. It all made sense—the oohs and ahhs from the studio audience, the "I'm not a professional actor" claims from the pitchmen—all of it.

My father confessed that he and my mother also used to scoff but have now purchased a myriad of timesaving, and perhaps even lifesaving, products this way. And like us, one night they were mocking the ignorant masses; then the next night, they looked at each other and simultaneously said, "Wow! We could use that!" Many of their friends and acquaintances have reported similar experiences, so apparently, there is an age everyone hits where all this stuff suddenly starts making sense. I understand that at that age, you also get an uncontrollable desire to book a few cruises too.

My wife and I have reached that age. There are times in the middle of the quiet night when I feel an overwhelming need for a knife that can cut a soda can in half. And just last month, Tami asked me if they still sell that Inside-the-Shell Egg Scrambler. Do you remember that one? It would scramble the egg right inside the shell. Tami said that it was really kind of cool, and I had to agree with her. Please note that even though this was a product my wife and I had previously scoffed at, we now thought we could use something like that. We did wonder who invented it, though. Was some guy scrambling an egg with a fork one morning when he swore to his exhausted self, "There has got to be a better way!" Then, for the next three months, he cut himself off from the world and stayed in his basement until one day when he walked upstairs and screamed, "Eureka!" (All inventors say that, don't they?) After "Eureka!" he probably shouted, "I have done it! Never again will I have to kill myself scrambling eggs. We will be rich!"(I always thought it would be neat to scramble an egg inside the shell and then incubate it. Perhaps this is where boneless chicken comes from.)

The Inside-the-Shell Egg Scrambler goes right along with the Popeil Pocket Fisherman. They've all sold millions, no doubt, but are there really that many impulse fishermen in the world? Who invented that one? Some guy just walking by a stream who said to himself, "You know, if only I had a fishing pole on me, I could catch some dinner. Eureka! I'll make a fishing pole that fits in my pocket!" Or maybe it was just a guy who heretofore had to carry his fishing pole everywhere he went and simply got tired of it poking people in elevators. Who knows?

Whoever's inventing all these products should be happy to know that my father and mother have all of them—the Ginsu knives, the Juice-Master, the chicken beer can barbecue roaster rack—all of it, right down to the Egg Scrambler. The chicken roaster was especially puzzling because neither one of them drinks beer.

And now, Tami and I have started collecting our own stash.

Tami leans more toward the exercise equipment. She just purchased the Body Flex, which looks to me like little more than a rubber band connected to a plastic pole. Personally, I think it's just the Pocket Fisherman pole with a rubber string attached to it. I can't say anything to her about it, though, because I would have to justify all the past purchases I've made at the Golf Channel to "shave strokes" off my game. Mathematically speaking, if all the strokes they told me I would "shave" off my game with these products actually came off, I would be shooting in the negative numbers. In reality, the only thing that got shaved off was a little bit of my dignity when I came out of the infomercial hypnosis and realized that just as batteries aren't always included with a product, neither is talent.

Still, if another infomercial comes along featuring another golf aid that promises to improve my game, I'll probably fall for that one too. Once I'm in the infomercial trance, all I can do is say, "I neeeeeeeeeeed one of those!"

So while I await the delivery of my RoboSweep, the Magna Hose, the Tuck It Bucket paint-roller cleaner and mop bucket and Tami awaits her latest order of Hairagami's Lé Loom, the Buttoneer, and a Pops-a-Dent, we continue watching our infomercials. For the most part, these products are pretty good. And anyway, what else can you do at two o'clock in the morning in a small town in Tennessee?

I do have one concern, though. This morning, Tami told me she wanted to keep the Pops-a-Dent on her keychain. That can't be a good sign.

"Pay attention, you stupid people!
Fools, when will you be wise?"
Psalm 94:8

CHAPTER FIFTEEN

Sorry, We're Going to Have to Disallow That Deduction

Those of you who truly know me know that I am not a wealthy man. I honestly believe what someone once told me—that if you divided up all of the wealth on the planet equally, in a matter of time it would be right back where it is now—not in my hands. Please understand that I am fine with living life in the red. Red happens to be my color, my "season," as they say. My wife, on the other hand, is of a different season. She prefers a little more green in her wardrobe and wallet. She likes to pay the bills on time and seems to take it personally when our ATM pretends it doesn't know us.

Like most "normal" people (her words, not mine), she would also like to have a few of the finer things in life: like a hot apple pie with her Big Mac. She'd also like furniture. Not a lot of it; just something to sit on while we're watching television. I have tried to tell her that the boys and I have more fun wrestling in the empty living room than we'd ever have just relaxing on a sofa (one that wouldn't even be ours until after thirty-six consecutive monthly payments). But she won't listen to this reasoning. She just sits there on the box in the middle of the living room and tells me I'm being narrow-minded.

That's why I'm coming to you.

Now, I have had some good years as a comedian and, hopefully, if you're reading this book and are not one of only six who actually paid money for it, I will have even more prosperity heading my way soon in the form of royalties. I'd even be happy just to have the advance paid back. But either way, I don't really worry about it. We have a roof over our heads, two cars in the garage, some nice clothes, and a Crock-Pot. What more could one family want? We're not rich, but we're comfortable. I'm not going to whine because I don't have an art collection (besides the masterpieces on the top half of our calendar pages), a jet ski, an SUV, or even the best golf clubs. (OK, I have whined a little about the golf clubs.) But overall, I realize we have the necessities of life, and, for me, that's enough.

I do understand my wife's point of view, however. We've been married for more than two decades, so furniture and a hot apple pie don't seem like a lot to ask for. I have even entertained the notion of going out and getting a new sofa or at least buying a jet ski with a really, really big seat that could double as a couch. But I haven't done it yet because as a bystander, I'm content. It doesn't take much to satisfy a bystander. We know that decorator furnishings would require too much involvement on our part. We'd have to be answering questions day in and day out.

"Should we put the armoire over here or over there?"

"Should we go with the marble or the plastic?"

"Is that a Rembrandt or Crayola?"

So I don't even go there. I'm happy with our home furnishings just the way they are: sparse, but paid for.

I haven't always been this easygoing about material things. When I was younger, I wanted to be independently wealthy. I would tell people all the time that I would be a millionaire someday. Then I would ask them if they'd like a hot dog with their Slurpee.

Looking back on my youthful desires, I don't believe I had the right motives. The main reason I wanted piles of money was to silence all those teachers who had described me as a bright kid who wouldn't amount to much because I had a bad attitude.

Bad attitude. Me? What a bunch of jerks! Actually, it wasn't that I had a bad attitude, I just had A. D. D., and try as I might, I just couldn't stay focused. But back in "the day," as I like to call it, teachers didn't care about syndromes such as A. D. D. They just thought you were acting up in class to get attention. They didn't realize that a force greater than you was driving you to get up and Riverdance on the cafeteria tables. You didn't mean to, you just couldn't fight the pull.

I can't tell you how many times I've been asked if I was the class clown at school. I always give the same reply, "I don't know if I was a clown, but the word *obnoxious* came up quite a bit."

To me, school was a chore that I couldn't wait to finish. My parents, like many parents of hyperactive A. D. D. children, got exhausted just trying to get me to pass each grade and eventually get a diploma. I must have heard a thousand times, "If you don't study hard and get good grades, you'll wind up a garbage man." What they neglected to tell me was that garbage men make eighty grand a year, and that isn't including all the neat stuff they get to retrieve from people's trash. So maybe that was an occupation to which I should have aspired.

In those days, though, I wasn't really aspiring to anything except getting into trouble. If memory serves me correctly, the faculty always pounded on me. I'm sure I deserved it, of course. My boundless energy was pretty disruptive in the classroom. So much so that whenever I was absent, the teachers would send a thank-you note to my parents.

One particular teacher, Miss Crandal, actually told me she hated me. She had gotten so frustrated with me that she dragged me out in the hall, slammed me against a locker, and screamed, "We all hate you, Jeffrey! Nobody wants you in their class." (No need to get out the tissues. I've been in therapy a lot of years, so I can talk about it now. The incident also helped my sense of humor grow, so I suppose I should be grateful.)

You see, Miss Crandal was a little overweight, so when she would shake me, her cheeks would vibrate and remind me of Jell-O. When you have A. D. D., it is hard not to focus on something wiggling around in front of you, so whilst she was slamming me and yelling at the top of her lungs, I couldn't help but laugh. And the more I laughed, the angrier she got. And the angrier she got, the more the Jell-O danced.

"Laugh at me?! Why, I'll take you down to the principal's office, you little punk!"

Then she would shake me some more and hold her breath, turning her cheeks a bright red.

"Raspberry!" I'd say. "That's the flavor. It's raspberry!"

For some reason, Miss Crandal never seemed to see or appreciate my budding talent for comedy. Instead, she would drag me down to the principal's office where my parents would be called, and then the whispering would begin.

"There's something wrong with that boy," she'd mumble under her breath. "He's *different*."

When my parents arrived, the principal would tell them that whilst my instructor was pummeling me, I had been muttering the word *raspberry* and laughing. Not being in on my inside joke, the staff felt that my uttering the name of a fruit for no apparent reason was a sure indicator of something seriously wrong with me.

Nobody had asked me why I had been laughing. If they had, they might have laughed too. And even if they didn't, I knew instinctively that jiggling raspberry Jell-O cheeks was a very funny sight.

I am confessing this here because my biggest fear is that on my deathbed I will gasp my final breath and croak out the word *raspberry*, forever leaving my kids with unanswerable questions.

"What's he saying?"

"Who knows?"

"It sounds like 'raspberry.'"

"Raspberry?"

"Yeah."

"You think he's nuts?"

"Well, at least it's verifiable now."

It's a shame that Orson Welles is no longer alive. My story might make a great follow-up to *Citizen Kane: Raspberry and Rosebud*—the double-disc DVD set.

When my time comes to say good-bye, world, good-bye, my family needn't worry because I am going to do everything in my power not to say, "Raspberry." I might say, "Hey, move over; you're stepping on my breathing tube!" but I won't say, "Raspberry." Last words should be far more poignant than a mention of fruit.

Another reason for sharing the story of Miss Crandal is to say that good grades and a wonderful school record are not the panacea for success as is touted. As Judge Smails from *Caddyshack* so eloquently said, "The world needs janitors too."

It also needs comedians who are driven to make the world laugh and content to live with no furniture.

One thing I can say about my financial situation over the years is that I've been consistent. I may not have made my million dollars yet, but I'm not in debtor's prison either. (What is a debtor's prison these days? The spot in front of the counter where you wait while the clerk enters your credit-card number for approval?)

God has used different situations throughout my life to teach me some very hard financial lessons. First and foremost, I've learned that despite all the television ads telling you how caring they are, most banks don't give a rat's tail about you or your family. They are not your friends. If you don't believe me, try calling your "friend" after you've missed a couple payments due to a death in the family and funeral expenses. They'll be so compassionate, they'll volunteer to swing by the funeral home to pick up your check.

The CEOs of banks and credit-card companies don't lie awake at night wondering whether you've had your daily supply of protein or if you're still licking crumbs out of the Fritos bag. They're in business to make money. So my financial rule number one is "Trust no 'friend' who feels justified in charging you two dollars to withdraw your own money from your own account at an ATM machine or 20 percent interest for the pleasure of doing business with them."

Rule number two is "Learn the importance of delayed gratification." That's something I have had a lot of trouble with. As a matter of fact, this was really going to be rule number six, but I couldn't wait. For those of you who aren't familiar with what delaying gratification is, let me just say that if all America learned how to do this, the balance and harmony that would result in our land would be heard around the world.

All right, who am I kidding? If America did that, the economy would go so deep into the abyss that the looting in the streets wouldn't get under control for years! So forget I even brought it up. Delaying gratification isn't something any of us should aspire to. Our economy needs our greed. If you want that new car, please don't wait until you actually have a job to pay for it. Tell yourself that if you had a new car, you would then be able to get a job. Get it now, pay for it whenever. That's what America is all about, right?

In the midst of my biggest spending spree back in the early nineties (which, I believe, was the number one contributing factor in getting the economy back on track), I did make one mistake. I somehow forgot to pay my taxes. Even a bystander has to pay his taxes. I say I forgot to pay them, but in reality, it was more along the lines of procrastination. Not a smart thing to do. The interest and penalties that the IRS charges are nothing short of freebooting (I really love my new thesaurus), and it's not like you can shop around for a better rate either. Of course, you can get a better rate from the Mafia . . . if they existed, that is.

I do have to say, however, that if you're a lonely person, the attention you will begin to receive from them can be nice. If you have no in-laws asking you how much you make, the IRS will be more than happy to fill in the gap. And they'll let you know just how much they care by corresponding with you by mail on a very regular basis, sending their greetings in large manila envelopes.

But because I am not a lonely person, after awhile, I came to hate those manila envelopes — really, truly hate them. I fretted over them every waking minute and dreamed about them every unwaking minute. They were my Nightmare on Twelfth and Constitution Street. I hated looking into my mailbox and seeing them. Finding a snake coiled up in there would have been a more welcome sight. At least snakes can only bite so much out of your hide.

I won't bore you with the details of my first two audits. They went relatively smoothly. I had to give them a few months' wages and a few minor organs, but otherwise, I was left unscathed. My third audit, however, is the one that I believe God Himself intervened in. Not that He came down and parted the 1040 forms, delivering me from their relentless pursuit. But He did part the waters of my stubbornness and pride and reminded me what the real promised land of life was.

Before I go on, I should say that I was not in a good place financially that year. Everything that I thought I valued had been taken away. One of my cars had been repossessed, my house was on the auction block, and my usually long-suffering wife was thinking hard about whether she wanted to remain married to a man obsessed with manila envelopes.

That was my mind-set when I walked in to the Internal Revenue Service building that day with my accountant, Van the

Tax Man (yes, that was his name—not exactly a high-powered accountant that Enron might use, but then again, he was cheap and didn't steal any money from me . . . and besides, he came highly recommended by the other patrons at the laundromat).

I took a number and was soon called into one of the auditor's offices. As Van and I sat down, I glanced around the room. This guy had every tax book the IRS has ever printed. I think he wanted to let us know that he meant business—you know, intimidate the little guy. But it was overkill. It was obvious we weren't exactly IBM coming in for an audit. I didn't have a tag team of tax-law specialists representing me. I just had Van, and if memory serves, it had taken him less than eight minutes to plug in my numbers on the tax forms. Even if I ended up owing what they said I owed, my little payment wasn't going to balance the national budget or even pay for a few presidential haircuts. I had no assets. I was, and still am, a stand-up comedian. As I've said before, we don't eat all that well. That's why so many of us are so angry.

"So how many days are you on the road?" the auditor asked.

"It's right on the form there," I said meekly.

"Oh," he said, then smirked and began explaining some obscure law on the tax books called the Transient Employee Law.

"What this law means in a nutshell," he said, "is that if you spend a certain number of days on the road, then your home is in essence the road."

Now my wife has told me that many times, but I was starting to sense that this line of reasoning wasn't going to land me in taxpayer paradise. It took about thirty seconds for me to figure out that he was trying to take away my home deduction. Saying that I lived on the road and not in my house would make a huge difference on my bottom line, so I asked as tactfully and respectfully as possible, "What pinhead created that law?"

I realize now that "pinhead" wasn't the politically correct term, but it was shorter than "nincompoop." In any event, he said the law was created because circus employees were taking advantage of the home tax law. They would buy houses and not live in them because they were on the road almost the whole year. In reality, their home was the road, and thus they were not legitimately entitled to the house deduction.

After he had fully explained his position, he sat back in his chair, satisfied. The smug look on his face was pricking at me like the forgotten toothpick in my pocket. I didn't want to, didn't mean to, but I lost it.

And that's when I believe God showed up.

Years later, after becoming a Christian, I would read about Jesus turning over the tables of the money changers, reminding me of this moment in the auditor's office, and I would mentally cheer Jesus on. "You tell 'em, Lord!" I'd say. I knew that Jesus' indignation was for an entirely different reason, but still, I believed I had experienced just a little of what He must have felt that day. Enough was indeed enough.

I turned to the smug little man on the other side of the table and said, "Circus employees?"

He nodded.

"Well, Lord knows the circus geeks are raking in the cash!" I said. (Disclaimer: If you're a circus geek reading this, I merely said that out of a sense of frustration, not superiority.)

The auditor just stared at me. So I continued. "Are you kidding me? What does biting the heads off of chickens make you these days?" (Not that I was considering a career change. And if you're a chicken or a chicken advocate reading this, please refer to the above disclaimer.)

I started ranting, venting every frustration that I had ever had with anyone in my entire life. That auditor got my ATM-fee wrath, my credit-card-interest wrath, my over-my-credit-limit-fee wrath, my telephone-solicitor-calling-me-during-dinner wrath—he got it all. And that's when it happened. A truth, a God moment, suddenly hit me. The only thing these people can take from me is my "stuff." That's it, my stuff. Everything else, and believe me it's the everything else that matters in life—my dignity, my peace of mind, my self-respect I didn't have to give them. They had no power to take the important things in life from me.

Reverend Tom Nelson once said that every so often "every man needs to get downwind from himself." That may not be something you'll find on a Hallmark plaque, but it's pretty powerful advice just the same. Well, it was at that moment that I finally paused long enough to get a good whiff of the kind of man I had been. I had let a stream of manila envelopes monopolize my attention and rob me of my joy and true blessings.

Despite what I thought, the "system" hadn't taken everything from me. I still had my wife, my kids, my dog, and some remnants of my dignity left. By life's accounting system, I was rich. Not rich enough to buy a hot apple pie for my wife at McDonald's, but I was rich in all the things that truly mattered.

I slid my key chain across his desk and said, "Go ahead, take it all. Everything I own. Load it up in a truck and drop it on the front lawn of the White House. I don't care."

And I meant it. That auditor showed me that there is strength in surrendering. As soon as I gave up what I was losing anyway, I regained power over my life. In trying to keep what I thought was important, I had been choking out everything that really did mean something to me. Sure, it is nice to have material things, but things will never love you back. Things won't greet you at the door when you come home from your "transient job." They can't put their arms around you and tell you how much they've missed you. In spite of the message we the people get every April fifteenth, we the people are what matters most. And I told my good uncle Sam that.

"Take it. You can have everything I own," I repeated. "I am through with you and your manila envelopes."

Rising to my feet, I motioned to Van the Tax Man that it was time for us to leave. Our business there was done. I didn't know how Van was going to spend the rest of his afternoon, but I was determined to go home and apologize to my wife and kids for the way I had been acting. I was going to repent of my manila obsession. I was going to be a new me.

When I walked out of the IRS building that day, it was indeed with a renewed sense of power. No longer did I fear what the system could do to me. I had surrendered, but I had also gained so much. I was once again the controller of my peace of mind, my happiness, and my priorities. I had made my stand and did not back down. No one would ever keep me from reaching my destiny ever again. I felt great!

Then I remembered I had to walk home.

*"Has any man planted a vineyard and
not begun to enjoy its fruit? Let him leave
and return home. Otherwise he may die in
battle and another man enjoy its fruit."*
Deuteronomy 20:6

CHAPTER SIXTEEN

This Is a CDC Nightmare

Children are walking petri dishes. You didn't hear that from Louis Pasteur. You heard it from me. And it's information you can take to the bank.

I have never been sick as often as I have since breeding children. Children not only carry every germ known to mankind, but kids' germs are far more potent than what we adults are carrying around with us. Germs will fester upon a young child's body for weeks at a time, growing into super germs until you end up with a drooling, gurgling biological weapon the Third World has yet to discover.

For further evidence, see the annual bulletins issued by the Centers for Disease Control in Atlanta, regarding seasonal dangers for us older people to peruse. Heading that list is the italicized caution to stay away from *anyone under the age of three.* It may not be worded in that exact way, but we all know what they mean. Researchers have figured out that underneath all that toddler cuteness is a terror hitherto seen only under a microscope in the most diabolical of experiments.

So we must consider ourselves duly warned. When the CDC speaks, a bystander/ hypochondriac such as myself tends to listen. I want to know about such dangers so I can do everything in my power to avoid them. In fact, that's the primary reason I quit napping in the open ranges of my living room. I've discovered that if I lie on my couch, the germ moguls disguised as my children will descend upon me quicker than Michael Moore on a Big Mac. Then there's the smell. All the baby powder in the world can't combat the odor a two-year-old with a cold is capable of emitting. I have never documented this, but I believe children actually sweat milk until they are about four or five years of age. When they're ill, their glands go into overdrive. These kids turn into a walking, breathing bowl of bubbling cottage cheese, and mark my words, it'll be the only time they won't fuss when they have to kiss you goodnight.

Another problem with napping out in the open is that my youngest can't seem to fight the temptation to crawl right up on to my rib cage and sit, gurgling and combusting and breathing a sound that registers somewhere between an obscene phone call and a moped on the decibel scale. He'll do this until I finally wake up. Then he'll lean forward and, thanks to gravity, everything in his pie hole will drop right on my face. The entrée is usually a combination of Ritz crackers and Hawaiian Punch, which when mixed makes some sort of quick-drying crimson caulk that only an industrial sandblaster or his mother's spit can remove.

Last week was the worst. Our youngest had something, but we weren't sure what it was. So I decided to limit my exposure and stay in my bedroom for most of the day. I must have fallen asleep because the next thing I knew I was being stirred to consciousness, not by the motor of my beloved child's breathing, but by the drip, drip, drip of drool falling from his lips. It was as if I had fallen asleep under a rain gutter.

Immediately, I became convinced that this exposure to God-knows-what would be the death of me. My pragmatic wife, always looking for the silver lining even in drool, thought that this germ onslaught would actually be good for me. Her reasoning was that every time I exposed myself to their germs, my immune system was getting the equivalent of a weight-lifting workout, so being bombarded with germs on a regular basis might very well be making me stronger, not weaker. Of course, the Creator hasn't told me or anyone else how many years of life I've been granted, so I have no way of proving whether anything I do is either extending or shortening my life.

So I decided to err on the side of caution. I was too tired and weak to lift the drooling little lad off of me, so I called out to anyone within earshot, "Someone come and get Curd Boy off me!"

As I awaited the arrival of my rescuer, the lad eyed my diet soda on the table, climbed off Mount Dad, toddled over to the beverage, and said, "Pease?" Now, as all fathers know, it is extremely difficult to turn down the combination of cuteness and manners. But I also know from past experience that once his lips touch my glass, the drink is no longer mine. It doesn't matter that he will politely offer it back to me; there will be a three-course meal floating on the top of it by then. And that's just the stuff I can see! My only prayer is that if I have to drink it, the corrosive effects of the cola, which have been known to eat through a penny, will dissolve any harmful microorganisms that were left behind by my little bio-toddler. Unlike me, the boy's older brother Aaron has no problem drinking after him. He doesn't care if there's an entire buffet floating on top; he just drinks around it, leaving behind his own three-course meal. Aaron does, however, draw the line at anything that has to do with diapers. He won't touch, straighten, or change a diaper. He will, however, be more than happy to give the household an environmental report whenever necessary. To quote this budding Shakespeare, "He stinketh!" And that brings me to this precious memory. I was on the phone one afternoon when Aaron, then a teenager, came downstairs in a panic. Bystanders don't like panic. It usually means we have to get involved, and by now, you know how I feel about that.

Teenagers live in a state of panic. It seems everything that happens to them is a do-or-die situation.

"DAD! DAD!" he screamed.

This could have been one of those times when I might have spent a few minutes trying to explain to my child that I was on the phone and that it is rude to interrupt me, but I was not in the mood to learn yet another lesson in futility. So I placed my hand over the receiver and asked, "What is it, son?"

"The baby had an accident in his pants and he's stinking up the whole house! All my friends are leaving!" Aaron wailed.

Naturally, "all my friends are leaving" is music to a bystander's ears. We long for our peace and quiet and feel violated if anyone deprives us of it. But apparently my son wanted his chums to stay and me to remove the baby from their presence.

But I didn't bite. Instead I asked Aaron when he thought his friends might be leaving, so I could decide on building an extension onto the house. He caught my sarcasm and didn't answer. Happy that I had made my point, I told him that I would handle the diaper matter after I was done with my telephone conversation.

"You might want to hurry," he interjected, "because he's taken the diaper off and is running around loose upstairs." That's the kind of message that will get even a bystander off the phone fast. I don't care if you're talking to the president of the United States, you would still stop in midconversation and say, "I'm sorry, Mr. Leader of the Free World, but Poop Boy is on the loose. I gots to go!" I hung up the telephone and headed upstairs, not knowing what kind of horror awaited me. But all the parenting classes in the world could not have prepared me for what I was about to witness.

Just as I reached the landing at the top of the stairs, I saw my toddler running down the hallway. I am not kidding you, this child was holding the diaper out in front of him and chasing my teenager's friends with it. The kid seemed to have an inherent sense that the weapon that he had in his hand was something the United Nations might want to know about, and he was now drunk with power. He ran after Aaron and his friends, laughing some kind of sick, twisted giggle, and out of nowhere came Ryan, holding a handful of the wet wipes, screaming, "You grab him, Dad! I'll wipe him!" To which I replied, "Are you crazy? I'm not touching that child! Herd him out onto the lawn and I'll hose him off!" As horrible as it was, I do have to admit at one point I was laughing pretty hard. We all were. That is, until he ran into my room and jumped up on the bed. Believe me, seeing Poop Boy on your new comforter will drain the funny out of any situation. But I didn't let him see my panic. I stopped laughing too. I've learned that if you laugh at these kinds of childish antics, the kid will think you're playing and just keep it up. So I had to play the adult (and believe me, that gets harder and harder every year). I had to execute my next move with the stealth of a second-story man. Any sudden motion might scare the boy into scooting across the comforter, and I have been married long enough to know that Tami would never believe me. I would be standing there like a moron, looking at her, pleading my case, and saying, "Are you nuts? The baby did that!"

To which she would reply, "My mother said you would get worse. I can't believe you would blame an innocent child who can't defend himself." Innocent child? Hardly.

So, not wanting the scene to escalate to that kind of severity, and even without donning a hazardous material suit, I approached him slowly, cautiously. I had to walk softly and carry a big wipey. It was either that or call out the Haz Mat team, and to tell you the truth, I don't think even they could have handled what that boy was packing. It was rough, but we managed to get through the decontamination process without further incident.

Kids. No wonder most of them outlive us.

———

"The boy sneezed seven times and opened his eyes."
2 Kings 4:35

CHAPTER SEVENTEEN

I'll Make a Man out of You Yet

Aaron came to me about four or five months ago and asked, "Could you build me a room in the basement?" I asked why he wanted this room, and he said that he needed "his space."

As a bystander, I can understand this. Bystanders love their space. But I knew there had to be more to his story. Basically, since the sixties, teenagers have used "I need my space" to cover the truth. What they're actually saying is, "You people really get on my nerves, but I have no money to move out, so how 'bout we put a floor between us?" I know this because I said the same thing to my father. He didn't offer me his basement though. His reply, if I remember correctly, was more like "You know, son, there's a lot of space right outside that front door."

My father wasn't one to mince words.

These "space expeditions" have been going on for years. In our youth, we all wanted the freedom that came with adulthood, only without any of the responsibility. We wanted the independence and none of the rules. After all, rules are far too constricting for eighteen-year-old "adults." At eighteen, we should be able to play our music as loud as we want, eat all the junk food our arteries can tolerate, and sleep in until the snooze alarm breaks from overuse. These yearnings for independence hit men harder because (I believe) we instinctively know that once we get married, a lot of this freedom is going to be surrendered. We only have a small window of opportunity to experience it, and that's why at eighteen, we're chomping at the bit.

I understand all of this, so I told my antsy heir that I would make a room in the basement for him, but that it was still his mother's and my house. That room wasn't to be mistaken for the freedom he sought. It would merely be a slight taste of it — a ween-er room, if you will, to guide him toward complete independence.

I don't think he heard anything I said, though, because a week or two after the room's completion, I was walking by the kitchen, once again just minding my own business, when I overheard Aaron on the telephone telling one of his adolescent little chums, "Hey, dude. I finally got my own place."

It was the "got my own place" that stopped me dead in my tracks. His own place? Who is he kidding? Since when did he become a cosigner to our thirty-year note? Sometimes I would like to get a true glimpse into how that boy processes information. I ran into my bedroom and told my wife, "That boy has no intention of ever leaving this house. He thinks I've built him a condominium down there, and we're just the upstairs neighbors he waves to every morning on his way to the unemployment office."

I decided to do the only thing I could do—freeze him out. I had a cousin who had some trouble getting rent from a tenant one winter, so he sealed the guy's vents shut. It cost him the coveted "Landlord of the Year" title, but eventually the guy paid up. I wasn't looking to collect rent from my son, I just . . . well, I guess I wanted my space too. I wanted him to realize that this was his parents' nest, not his, and, as a single guy, he would have much more fun on his own. I also needed the refrigerator to stay stocked more than three hours after a $200 trip to Kroger. But I digress.

As long as my son thought of that place in the basement as his pad with kitchen and laundry privileges, neither of our goals would be met.

My dad made this same point to me years ago. Only he did it in his own way. Dad's favorite saying was that he was going to make a man out me. His method of choice was hunting. I have to say, I don't understand hunting. I don't have any moral reasons against it; I just don't get it. Perhaps I would enjoy it more if pizzas flew, but the fact that they don't keeps me from spending my weekends dressed like a tree and shooting at the sky. (It also keeps pepperoni off my windshield.)

Maybe the reason I didn't enjoy the sport was my hunting assignment. Whenever my father, my brother Kirk, and I went hunting, my assignment was to be the dog. Not that I hung my head out the car window and let my hair and tongue flap in the wind or anything like that (I only did that twice); my job was to walk ahead of everybody and flush the wild critters out of the bush whilst a bunch of drunken rednecks fired twelve gauges over my head. Ah, family togetherness. Don't you love it? I was the only eight-year-old kid in my neighborhood that got combat pay added to my allowance.

If that weren't bad enough, the ride to the hunting grounds was also brutal. My dad would pack me in the car with my brother and six of his closest buds. We were jammed in so tight, if we'd had a car wreck, none of us would bleed. And because it was winter, all the windows had to be rolled up. This is not a good situation, if you get my whiff, I mean, drift. If you've ever been around grown men in the early morning hours, you know they can sound like a '68 Barracuda with a bad intake valve. By the time we got where we were going, there was enough methane in that car to blow up a Third-World country. And the way my father's friends reacted to the experience, you would have thought it was nitrous oxide. They couldn't stop their laughfest for the rest of the day.

Even with all of that, I might have been able to tolerate the hunting excursions a little more if my older brother didn't always get to shoot a gun. I'm not ashamed to admit that I was jealous and didn't understand why Kirk got to do that and I didn't. It couldn't possibly have anything to do with aim. Not only could my brother miss the broadside of a barn, he could miss the entire county the barn was in. He couldn't hit a redneck at a tractor pull. He couldn't hit a liberal at a Barbra Streisand concert. Or a toupee at a quartet convention. Well, just pick one; I have to move on. So in three years of hunting, my brother only hit one thing he had aimed at — a rabbit. He not only hit it once; he emptied his twelve gauge into that poor little ball of fur. Talk about excessive force. He got so excited, you would have thought he'd just bagged a grizzly. I asked him why he felt the need to plug Ol' Bugs full of shells, and he said, "I don't know. I guess I just panicked." That was understandable. We all know how fierce and threatening a bunny can look hopping down the bunny trail.

Another thing I never understood about hunting was the clothing. My father would dress us in fatigues and put weeds in our hats and dirt on our faces. The point was to make us look as much like a bush as we could. Evidently, that's one of the rules of hunting. But come on now, do hunters really think this charade actually fools a deer in his own 'hood? I can't see Bambi strolling through the woods and stopping every so often to say, "Hmm. Another set of bushes wearing gym shoes? Nothing odd about that."

Truth is, more deer are killed in America by automobiles than by hunters. So the obvious question is, why are hunters dressing like shrubbery when they should be dressing like Volvos? It wouldn't take but a couple of headlights and a salt lick stuck on their forehead. Instead of hiding out in the forest, risking ticks, all they'd have to do is stand by the deer-crossing sign on the highway. (By the way, how does the deer know that's where he's supposed to cross? Will a gaggle of deer walking out of the woods actually stop at that sign, read it, then hesitate while the head deer turns around and yells, "Everybody back! This is a yield.")

One thing I will say about my dad is that when it came to hunting, he didn't just hunt one species. He was an equal-opportunity game hunter. He hunted everything with four legs.

The year we went moose hunting in upper Michigan is yet one more story that I'll never forget. For this, not only did I get my G. I. Joe uniform, but my father also gave me a special horn to blow. I asked him why I needed a horn, and he said (are you ready for this?), "It's the mating call of a moose, boy."

Now I have to admit, I was pretty naive in those days. To me, it was just a horn. I didn't realize by blowing it, I was playing Bullwinkle's version of *The Dating Game.* When I got a little older, I started wondering, "What if that moose horn had actually worked?" How does one assuage twenty-two-hundred pounds of amorous bull moose?

Luckily, I wasn't a very good moose horn player either.

I can still recall coming home after a day of hunting. My mother would be standing at the door as we got out of the car and would always ask the same question, "How was hunting, boys?" To which I would usually reply, "It was great, Mom! Kirk mutilated a rabbit, Dad bagged a deer, and I got a date for the prom."

My point in telling you all this, and yes, I do have one, is that every father has his own way of teaching his children lessons about life. Some fathers teach their offspring these lessons at a NASCAR racetrack. Others teach it on the football field or while working on the family farm. My dad did it in the woods with a gun in one hand and fresh game in the other. The important thing isn't how our dads taught us about life; the important thing is that they did.

Now I have sons of my own, and it's time for one of them to go out into the world and become his own person. As a father, I know he needs freedom to mature into a responsible adult. I know he only has that small window of time to enjoy his independence and his youth before he meets the girl of his dreams and settles down. He needs to make his own decisions, his own mistakes, and yes, his own money. It's like how God is with us. He wants us to grow up in our faith—to quit our whining, self-centered laziness and get on with our calling.

I wanted Aaron to get on with his calling. Staying in the safety of the nest wasn't doing him, or his mother and me, any good. So last winter, I did what I said I would do four months earlier. I sealed the vents in his room. It took a couple of days, but he finally did come upstairs. The scene was like one of those Norman Rockwell paintings, only more like real life. There he was, wrapped in an electric blanket with two hundred feet of orange extension cord trailing behind him. Shivering, he asked, "Hey, what's with the heat?"

"I don't know," I said. "Why don't you talk to your home-owner association, Condo Boy?"

Then I unplugged him.

It's OK. Utilities were never included in the original arrangement.

"Take your [hunting] gear, your quiver and bow, and go out in the field to hunt some game for me."
Genesis 27:3

CHAPTER EIGHTEEN

Dr. Phil Says

The Bible tells us that the meek will inherit the earth, but we live in a world where the opposite seems to be true much of the time. To be heard in today's society, you need to be louder than everyone else. It's survival of the mouthiest.

Still, Mother Teresa was pretty meek and soft-spoken and she managed to be heard all right. She did it without having her own talk show, megaphone, or a telemarketing campaign. Mother Teresa made herself heard not by volume but by example. She was a treasure hunter, finding value in what society threw away. Not clothing or furniture, but discards of the human kind.

There wasn't anything glamorous about Mother Teresa's life work. She did it without a lot of glory or fanfare. She helped those who could in no way return her kindness. She had no ulterior motives. She didn't do charity work so people would notice her goodness. She didn't give so others would be indebted to her. She just loved and gave for no other reason than it was the right thing to do.

In the end, when the pope paid a special tribute to Mother Teresa, a quarter of a million people showed up for the privilege to be part of the celebration. A quarter of a million people! All paying tribute to a lady who couldn't do it all but did what she could. Mother Teresa didn't sit around waiting for a record deal or a movie role to make her impact on the world. She simply worked with what she had where she was. She took to heart what the Bible asked her to do. She loved. Any glory that this world tried to bestow upon her was sent right back to her Lord and Savior, Jesus Christ. She was gentle, yet she earned the respect of millions. She was quiet, but she gained the attention of the whole world. To this day, her name is one of the most recognizable names in religion, and she did it all without a publicist.

Mother Teresa was the meek inheriting the earth, personified.

Countless other faithful servants of all types work around the world, doing the same thing Mother Teresa did—loving people. These are bright, articulate men and women who could have made a comfortable living in our society. They could have climbed the corporate ladder with the rest of us but chose to answer a higher calling and take a road less traveled and far less celebrated.

But don't confuse meek with weak. It took a lot of courage for Mother Teresa to stand up for her beliefs. And it takes courage for us to stand up for our beliefs too. In a discussion on anything about the human condition, try interjecting a "You know, the Bible says . . ." and see what happens. Often, what you'll hear next is the simultaneous slamming shut of a dozen previously open minds. Some people aren't as inclusive as they think they are, are they?

On the other hand, toss out a "Dr. Phil says . . ." and everyone leans forward to hear what pearls of wisdom are going to
drop from your lips. It's as if E. F. Hutton himself is speaking.

Truth is, Dr. Phil is basically saying the same thing that has
been said a thousand times, hundreds of years ago. Except for
a few fashion trends, not a lot has changed over the years.
Couples still bicker over finances, teenagers still rebel against
their parents, mothers-in-law still criticize sons-in-law for
existing, and inconsiderate neighbors still leave their broken-
down vehicles on their lawns (they've just changed from char-
iots to Chevys).

As enlightened as we like to think our society has become,
we still have a long way to go. It's not that we don't try. We just
aren't going about it in the most effective way. We look everywhere to fix ourselves except the one place that withstands the
test of time—the Bible. The shelves at our bookstores are full
of man's attempts to reach nirvana. Dr. Phil is just the latest in
a long list of soon-to-be-forgotten gurus whom we look to for
the answer to all our problems.

Recently, Dr. Phil turned his genius toward weight loss. If
you ask me, that's a little like me doing a golf instructional
video. Not that Dr. Phil is out of shape and has nothing important to offer the overweight. I'm sure he does. But even though
I'm not that bad of a golfer, I know I'm not Tiger Woods.

"Hey, I'm Jeff Allen. I can't break eighty myself, but I'm
going to tell you how to do what I wish I could do but can't."

I'd sell nine copies to my relatives. And three of them
would want their money back.

Maybe Dr. Phil is merely opening the floodgates for the
"new expert." We could start seeing infomercials touting

Elizabeth Taylor marriage seminars, Mike Tyson's anger management classes, and perhaps even a Martha Stewart How to Succeed on Wall Street video series.

So why is it that we'll accept everyone else's opinions on life but say it's old-fashioned or irrelevant when someone suggests looking in the Bible for answers? Where's our open-mindedness when it comes to God?

As I'm writing this, there is talk of educating first-graders on the concept of tolerance. I have no problem with teaching the next generation to be more tolerant of others. I've also encountered plenty of intolerant children myself when my golf balls have hit their little heads. (That'll teach them to stand behind me.)

So it's not tolerance that I have a problem with. What I have a problem with is selective tolerance. Are our children being taught tolerance for all human beings or just the ones with a strong lobbying group?

It is difficult even for a bystander not to see the hypocrisy in a tolerance policy that shows so little tolerance for anyone who disagrees with it. Take the topic of creation, for example. Teachers and professors can sometimes treat a student who believes in creation as if she just beamed down from the planet Lulu. But evolution has never been proven as fact, so why all the scientific arrogance? If you want my opinion, the only similarity I've ever found between man and ape is that we both hate to shave.

When evolution was first being introduced into our school curriculum, we were told that the evolutionists merely wanted their theory to be taught along with creationism. But I wonder how many teachers are still bothering to teach creationism? In some schools the "theory" of evolution has been elevated to fact, without having the facts, and creationism, the basis for belief in God of the overwhelming majority of the population, is scoffed at.

And to those handful of celebrities who feel compelled to share their political views with the rest of us, most of us don't really need to hear about your politics. We just want you to do what you do best: act, sing, or play a musical instrument. I don't need you to tell me how to vote. Don't take it personally. I don't want my car mechanic telling me how the country should be run either. I'm only in a hurry to get my car back on the road. I don't want the guy at the fast-food counter giving me investment advice; I just want my burger. I have friends and family and business associates whom I can debate politics and other subjects with whenever I care to. I also have newspapers, news magazines, and television news programs at my disposal. And when all else fails, I think I might even be able to make up my own mind about such things.

Now, you're probably saying to yourselves, "Hey, why doesn't the comedian just shut up then and heed his own advice? Who said we want to hear his opinion?"

All right, you win; I'll shut up about these matters.

Weeeeeeeeeell, I was going to shut up, but I am writing this the day after the Super Bowl. You know the one, the one where Janet Jackson and Justin Timberlake took what people do in private and made it public. The enormous public outcry that came after that halftime surprise reminded the entertainment moguls once again that there are a lot of people living between New York and Los Angeles who might not appreciate that sort of thing happening in front of their six-year-olds.

Don't get me wrong. This is not about people who've made a bad judgment call and did or said something they regret now. We've all done that. This is about boundaries. It's about standing up when we have to and being quiet when we need to. It's about having respect for all opinions, not just the ones most in tune with our own. It's about knowing what we can live with and what we can't.

I love the term "fabric of society." It lets me picture my life as a sort of garment that I wear. The choices I make on a daily basis are the fabric of the coat. The principles that guide my life are the seams that hold it all together. I cannot separate my choices from my principles without ripping the coat apart. If I did, my life would be fragmented and disoriented, leaving me hopeless. Without principles to guide my decisions, I am unprotected and naked as I try to navigate my way through a cold world.

It wasn't until Christ captured my heart that I began to understand the importance of humbly recognizing a higher authority. It took the weight of the world off my shoulders and put it back where it belonged—on the shoulders of the One who created both it and me. How arrogant it was of me to ever think I could do this thing called life on my own.

But I had to change my way of thinking. I had to learn that the only how-to book that is going to last is God's Word, and it hasn't changed in thousands of years; unlike the scientific community, which seems to be constantly changing its beliefs.

And I don't even want to get into how many times science has changed its mind on what we should eat. This is why I chuckle at the "new ideas" Dr. Phil and others like him tout because in the big picture, what they have to say will one day wind up right next to this book on someone's lawn at a garage sale. The only thing that will outlast us all—you, me, Dr. Phil, and the rest of the world—is faith.

———

"He put a new song in my mouth,
a hymn of praise to our God."
Psalm 40:3

CHAPTER NINETEEN

I Believe It's My Turn, Pastor

I think it was Sigmund Freud who spent most of his practice delving into a person's childhood, looking for the keys to unlock the treasure chest of that person's soul. It was either Freud or SpongeBob. For the sake of argument, we'll say it was Sigmund. I also believe it was his contemporary Carl Jung who stated that we spend our childhoods gathering up things and putting them into a big psychic bag that we lug around with us day in and day out until the weight of it gets to be too much. Then we spend our entire adulthoods emptying the bag.

If philosophers and psychologists really want to understand the human condition, they should read Ecclesiastes. When it comes to understanding humanity, Solomon knew his stuff. He is often referred to as the wisest man who ever lived. He's the guy who set the bar higher for all the rest of us.

But then, maybe SpongeBob has too.

Years ago, I read about a method where a psychologist asks a first-time patient about his earliest childhood memory. From the patient's response, the psychologist is able to determine a major key to the individual's arrested development.

I don't know if that technique is valid, but after reading about it, I started thinking about my earliest memory. After all these years, it's still as vivid as it ever was. I was standing on second base in a Little League game, waving for my parents to look at me. Of course, the ball had just been hit and I was supposed to be running on to third, but I had my priorities. I was there for the attention.

So if there is truth to this earliest-memory theory, then my standing on stage and telling jokes is merely a desire to have people look at me. Some might think that I did not get enough attention as a child. But how can that be? Every morning my mother couldn't wait to see me. She would stand at my bedroom door for an hour or so just begging me to get up.

My mother wasn't always in the best of moods in the morning. I'm sure it must have had something to do with those jumbo rollers she always slept in. Remember those? They were the size of toilet paper rolls, and women rolled their hair in them, then tried to sleep with their neck six inches off the pillow. Try sleeping like that every night and you'd wake up a little cranky too.

But I got more attention than just when my mom was trying to get me up in the morning. My brother, Kirk, loved me so much he couldn't seem to keep his hands off me. His idea of an entertaining Saturday night was to get me alone in the dark, turn on some Vincent Price horror flick (I watch those now and can't imagine what a wimp I was to be so scared), and then, when I least expected it, he'd grab me by the throat and scream. If I started crying, he would laugh like it was the funniest thing in the world. Then he'd do it all over again.

So you see, I had plenty of attention.

I can't really blame my brother for picking on me. I know I did plenty of things that bugged him—like throwing that pack of firecrackers under his bed while he was slumbering. Even though this is not a good example of brotherly love, my brother still wanted to hug me afterward. I think that's why he chased me for two blocks. It was only when he was standing in the middle of the street, vowing revenge, that he realized he was wearing only his underwear.

Embarrassed, he went home to taunt me another day. Of course, I would act relieved. But I wasn't really ever scared of him. After all, some guy screaming about how he's going to tear out your lungs and beat you over the head with them doesn't carry a whole lot of weight when he's standing there in a pair of Scooby-Doo underwear.

I've often wondered what my brother would have done if he didn't have me to pound on. I had to have been a major part of his purpose for existence. I certainly played a major role in his daily workout program. His routine was to bench-press ten Jeffs every morning before getting ready for school.

I don't remember what age I was when his brotherly smackdowns stopped, but it might have been around the time I topped out at six-two and about 180 pounds. I wasn't quite so easy to scare with old Vincent Price movies then. The change was sudden. One day he was sitting on me, apparently trying to hatch another skull for me, and the next day he wasn't.

Some of the best times I have had since leaving my parents' house have been sitting with my family and just reminiscing about stories like these. I don't know why, but the funniest ones usually come from the most painful memories. I am not sure, but I believe it was Woody Allen who said that comedy is tragedy plus time. What that means is that if a person has time to heal from his wounds, the least he should be able to do is find some humor in them. That's his outer reward for inner pain.

Stories also keep history alive. Most of our family history is whatever our parents have told us (assuming it's true — some parents rewrite history) because we were too young to remember the tales ourselves. Like comedian Rick Reynolds said, "I am always amazed when I get together with my family how our Kafkaesque-like childhood has somehow been rewritten into a Frank Capra move." So telling stories is not only fun but necessary.

I have my own children today, and they are making memories that they'll pass down to their children. Now that Aaron is grown, I like nothing more than sitting with him and reliving Aaron stories.

One of our family's favorites happened when he was six years old and just starting kindergarten. And yes, I do have his permission to share this.

The school bus used to let Aaron off right in front of our home, but instead of the Beav's method of walking into the house and sharing the happenings of his day with Ward and June, Aaron would bolt past us to the bathroom. This went on for a couple of weeks. He'd get off the bus then sprint to the bathroom. I have to admit there were times when, just for kicks, Tami and I would play Ward and June and try to ask him about his day, blocking his way to his destination, but he wasn't having any of it.

One day, while we were standing in the hall, we heard the bus pull up out front, and as usual, we waited for the Bullet to come shooting past us. But the Bullet never came. We waited a little longer, then a little longer, but still no Aaron. I walked outside just in time to see him coming out of the woods behind us, zipping up his pants and picking up his backpack from where he had apparently dropped it.

Being the skilled detectives that we were, Tami and I deduced from the scene that the little guy had run into the forest to do his business, obviously wanting to circumvent the Cleaver interference that he was accustomed to encountering. But what we didn't know until later was that to tidy himself up, he had used leaves — and not just any leaves. Unbeknownst to him, my son had traded Charmin for poison ivy.

It didn't take long for Aaron's little body to tell him what a bad idea that trade had been. He broke out in a rash from bow to stern, and needless to say, he was miserable. It wasn't easy on us either. We had to watch him waddling down the hallway and try our best not to laugh at the humor of it all. Eventually, he was able to laugh too. And like I said, it's one of our favorite family stories.

Stories are an important part of our lives. They put things into a historical context. They capture moments as a gift to future generations. They let your children know that not only were you paying attention but you also enjoyed their presence enough to remember the details. And *enjoy* is the key word here. Stories say you enjoyed your kids.

Another family anecdote involves our son Ryan. It had to do with the same topic; only he was a lot younger and hadn't even completed Potty Training 101. Now, as many of you know, one of the more trying times that parents have to endure is attempting to potty-train their little darlings. There are already a number of books on the market, sharing tips for accomplishing this necessary feat, so I won't bore you with the how-to dynamics. I will, however, give you the how-not-to dynamics.

Ryan was a little different from Aaron in that he didn't like other people looking at him sans clothing. When Aaron was little, he used to walk down the hall without a stitch of clothing on and give the commuters on their way to work something to chat about. On the other hand, if Ryan was in the bathroom even in the middle of doing his business, and you happened to walk by and glance in, he would walk over, still doing his business, and close the bathroom door. My wife said he was shy. But I don't see how that could be because one evening during a dinner party we were hosting, this same precious child wandered in our dining room, stark naked, then walked over to one of our guests, held out a roll of toilet paper, and said, "Wipe, pease!"

That's enough to make guests repossess their hostess gifts. I mean, what in the world do you say to that? "More stuffed mushrooms?"

I ended up saying the only thing I could say, "Here, I believe it's my turn, Pastor."

(And he thought the mission field would have been the tougher assignment!)

I excused myself from the table, took the little lad by the hand, and led him out of the room, saying, "Wave bye-bye to these nice people, son. I'm sure they will never be in our home again."

I'm saving that one to tell at his wedding.

My parents love telling the story about me and how stubborn and pigheaded I was as a child. Tami has a few of these stories herself, but I'm already getting close to my required word count, so I won't bore you with them. I will, however, share my parents' story.

You have to understand that as a child I was always running away from home. It was usually after my brother had pounded on me, or on report card day, or after my brother had pounded on me on report card day. It doesn't really matter what provoked it; all I know is I had usually "had enough."

I would pack a bag and hop onto my bike and leave all those people, never to return again.

About two or three blocks away, "never" seemed like a pretty long time, so I would turn around and head back home. I may have been a rebel, but I was still a bystander, and bystanders don't run away from home. We prefer to sleep in our own beds and have food and television at our disposal.

Our neighbors, who weren't bystanders, would always get involved in my escapes, laughing at me as they saw me riding by in a huff.

"What exotic place are you running away to today, Jeff?" they would ask, knowing that I would be making the return trip in just a few minutes. Sometimes I'd answer something like Fiji or Morocco or some other paradise where only mosquitoes bugged you, not big brothers. But most of the time, I just ignored them.

I'm not sure why, but I always seemed to run away on days my father wasn't home. I figured he would try to stop me from venturing off into the vast and wild unknown. But apparently, I was wrong.

It was a cold December, even cold for Chicago, and although my father was home, I had "had enough" again and was ready to take to the road. I told everyone that I really, really, really meant it this time.

Somehow word had reached him that I was indeed running away, and this time it would be for good. Dad walked into my bedroom as I was packing my suitcase, the one he and my mother had bought me for Christmas. (By the way, what parent buys his eight-year-old a suitcase for Christmas? Maybe I was too blind to see it then, but was that a hint?)

My father didn't seem to be bothered by my leaving. (Did I mention that this time I really meant it?) He just sat down on the edge of my bed and watched me.

"So you're leaving us, huh?" he asked.

"Yeah," I said. "This was the last straw!" I was, of course, too young to even understand that phrase, and I remember wondering where all the other straws had gone if I was down to my last one, but for once I didn't get off message.

"I'm running away!" I said. "And no one's gonna stop me!"

Dad didn't flinch. He just calmly said, "You know, I understand how much of a pain it can be living here, and I certainly don't want you to have to bear anymore than you desire to. So if you want to leave, you can."

I didn't care how much he begged me to stay, no matter how much he told me it would hurt him, no matter how much he . . . wait a minute. Did he just say I could go?

Wow. Apparently, Dad knew I meant business. He wasn't about to toy with someone as determined as I was. He knew I was making no idle threat. I was really running away this time. There wasn't anything anyone could do or say to stop me.

And with that, Dad turned to walk out of the room.

"Really?" I called after him, testing him. "'Cause this time I mean it! I really mean it! I am going to go as far away from here as I can get!"

Again, there was no reaction, except "OK." Then he poked his head into my room again and said, "But I did happen to notice that you're packing a few things in that suitcase—you know, the one we bought you for Christmas instead of a cool toy because we like to crush your little dreams for our own personal entertainment."

All right, that's not what he said when he poked his head into my room. It just sounded like that. What he really did say was that everything in that suitcase belonged to him and he would like to have it all back before I left.

"Fine!" I said. "This stuff just weighs me down anyway!"

I took everything out of the suitcase, put it all on the bed, and then tried to walk past him and out my door.

"Whoa, wait a minute," he said, temporarily blocking my path. "I believe the clothes you're wearing were also given to you by me. I'd also like those back before you go."

"Fine!" I said. "I don't like them anyway." So I took off all my clothes down to my underwear. When I make a point, I really make it.

As I started to leave again, Dad stopped me one last time.

"I believe I gave you the underwear you're wearing too. Just think of me as the repo man. Hand 'em over."

All right, now I was really being tested. But this bystander had taken all he could take and there was no backing down now. I had drawn a line in the sand. I took off the underwear and, standing there au naturel, said, "Can I go now?"

"Yes," my father said calmly. "You are now as you came into this world to me, naked. You may leave as you came. Good-bye. Call us when you get there."

I knew he didn't think I'd do it, and of course, that just made me more determined to run outside into what was probably a windchill of -10 degrees. But I didn't care. This time I was really, really running away. I raced through the snow until my mother finally caught up with me two blocks from home and literally dragged my naked little body back to the house. I was kicking and screaming the whole way, but when we arrived home, my father just laughed and said, "Where were you going to go, boy? I can't believe you actually left the house like that. You are the most stubborn, pigheaded child I have ever seen."

Considering the fact that it took me two hours to warm up my blood enough to be considered mammal, he might have had a point.

After that night, my mom took everyone in the family off to the side and told them to be nice to me because I had a screw loose. And maybe she was right. But if I did have a screw loose, it had to have been because my brother knocked it away during one of his brotherly wrestling matches. But looking back on them now, even they were fun.

The truth is every family has its stories—funny, sad, moving, inspirational stories. Stories of faith and vulnerabilities. Stories of pain and hope. Stories that will be forever lost if we don't tell them to future generations.

Tell your stories.

---

*"Though I have many things to write to you,
I don't want to do so with paper and ink.
Instead, I hope to be with you and talk face to
face so that our joy may be complete."*
2 John 1:12

CHAPTER TWENTY

Help Me, Mr. Wizard

Throughout this book I have shared with you my lifelong attempt to spend my days as nothing more than a bystander. "Don't get involved" has been my motto since day one. If I don't get involved, I won't be affected.

But as I've grown older, I have begun to notice that everything in this life seems to have an effect on me, directly or indirectly, whether I want it to or not. I can choose to not get involved with the man in front of me who's trying to persuade the bank teller to count out his four thousand pennies by hand; but the fact that he's making me late for my meeting sucks me straight into his problem against my will. I can choose to stay above the fray of politics, but when one side starts making hypocritical statements, I can't help but want to chime in with my two cents' worth, even if it's only to the television screen. In fact, I believe I may be the one who actually started interactive TV. I've been talking to political analysts whom I disagree with for years in the same way I used to talk to sportscasters and referees during sporting events.

"Are you blind?!"
"That was a foul!"
"He's safe!"
"Where's a referee when you need one?"
"Throw de bum out!"

As a kid growing up in Chicago, I loved sports. But I wasn't just a spectator or fan of sports; I was a player too. Players can't be bystanders. They have to be involved. And win or lose, their hearts are 100 percent with their teams. They don't sit on the sidelines and read magazines, looking up every so often just to see how much time is left on the clock. They fully participate.

Professional players even put down roots and raise their families in their team's cities. They make an investment in their communities and aren't so quick to want to be traded out. This means the townspeople get to know them year in and year out. I can still recite the starting lineup from the 1968 White Sox team, and I wasn't even a White Sox fan. I was a Southside boy. I loved the Cubs, which meant I got to fight for years with my friends who were Cubs fans over which team was better, the Cubs or the Sox. The arguments were always moot because both teams were usually mathematically eliminated by the all-star break every year anyway. But we defended our teams with every fiber of our beings. And that's the definition of a fan—an emotional participant. Fans never give up hope for their team. If not this game, then the next. If not this season, then the next. If not this lifetime, then, well, you get my drift.

Being a sports fan in Chicago also gave me my first lesson in true humility. We didn't get to have a lot of celebrations, but that was all right. You didn't stay a fan of one of Chicago's teams because they won championships. You did it out of pure unadulterated love . . . and loyalty . . . and boundless hope. Like the dogwoods, hope would be reborn within each of us every year, and we would begin the year arguing with fervor about how good our respective teams were.

By July, though, the humidity and reality had begun to dampen both our clothes and our spirits. Things were looking so bleak for our baseball teams that all we could do was reassure them that we'd be there for them the next time, and then we'd start looking forward to football season. No matter what they say, this is the primary reason Chicagoans love the change of seasons. It shortens our pain.

The cool thing about our football season was that there was only one team in Chicago: "Da Bears." The majority of us guys became a united force behind the Bears, and we'd gang up on the one Packers fan among us. Every group has their Judas Iscariot. Ours was my buddy Haggard. (I'm not sure what his parents were thinking when they named him, but something tells me they were tired.) Anyway, it was considered sacrilegious for a Chicagoan to root for the Packers, but Haggard was not into Scripture. He just wanted to root for a "winning team," as he told us day in and day out. He never understood or appreciated the character that the rest of us were developing as we suffered along with the Bears season after season after season. Let Haggard have his winner's pennants; we were learning how to lose with dignity, and that's something his childhood never afforded him.

Yes, we were a loyal lot. The Bears were our team. My team. I lived through Abe Gibron, Jack Concannon, and who could ever forget Bobby Douglas, who threw every pass as hard as he could. Man, could he throw! He could throw a pass eighty yards on a rope! Problem was, he threw *every* pass eighty yards, regardless of where his teammates happened to be at the moment. It was because of these players and others like them that we would enter each new season full of hope. Every Sunday we would sit with our cheese fondue and soda pops, and we would live and die with the Bears. They'd lose and we'd hang on. They'd lose again and we'd still hang on. This went on every Sunday until about the middle of October—when we could no longer deny the truth. The Bears didn't have a chance. Our season was over. We would still watch the games, but our chins and our Bears pennants would be dragging on the floor.

Despite our loyalty, there were a few times when bitterness would begin to seep in and the jokes would start. As they say, you tease the ones you love. But the sarcasm would only last until basketball and hockey season started, and then we were back rooting for our home teams. I was a Bulls fan long before Michael Jordan ever showed up and a Black Hawk fan in the days when Keith Magnuson not only left his heart on the ice, but also a few teeth.

As any sports fan knows, following a team takes a huge emotional investment. You hope, you pray, you spend your money on overpriced hot dogs and soda; you watch, you cheer, you moan; in other words, you are emotionally invested in every game and each new season. But like a disillusioned but still hopeful lover, you learn to simply enjoy the hype and the promises while lowering your expectations just a tad. You love your team but come to accept the fact that they're fallible. You remain loyal but don't ignore reality while you're at it. You're hopeful for the future but not blind to the present. Even in our worst years, there was a common bond among us fans as we stood in the stands and watched yet another Super Bowl chance come and go. We didn't quit, just like we didn't expect them to quit. The true fan is one who goes out to the ballpark in September, long after his team has been eliminated from any postseason opportunities. The true fan knows there are still good plays to see, good seats to enjoy, and good hot dogs to be digested again and again.

What I am trying to say is, it takes work and an investment of time to reap the full rewards of any relationship. I haven't learned much in my bystander life, but I have learned this — committed love cuts deep. In the midst of hopelessness, it refuses to give up hope; in the midst of whatever life throws at it, it never dies away.

Last October, the Chicago Cubs were in the League Championship Series for the first time in years. They were everyone's favorite to win and go to the World Series. That's nothing short of a miracle.

But their true fans knew they had it in them all along.

Now, I hadn't watched a Cubs game in over ten years, and anyone who follows these things knows all too well that the Cubs had a meltdown in the seventh inning of the sixth game, so as you can imagine, it was sad for me to watch. At one point my wife walked into the room and asked if I wanted to talk about it. I just took it like any other man watching one of his favorite teams lose would. I curled up in the fetal position and wept. That team's loss opened up every childhood wound that the teams of the sixties and seventies had inflicted upon me. I sat there, gutted like a trout, hoping against hope that they could pull out of it. But when the Cubs blew the seventh game, I knew I was at a crossroads. Would I finally and forever abandon this team and the teams of my childhood that had brought me so much grief over the years? Or would I remain steadfast, loyal, and committed to the end?

Like any true sports fan, I made a conscious decision to stick by my teams, win or lose. They need me most when they're down. That's not the time to cut loose and run. I still marvel, though, at how even after all these years, these teams continue to have the power to inflict such pain on me.

It's great to be in love, isn't it?

Today, I am still watching the Cubs. I will follow them all season until the play-offs, or until they are once again mathematically eliminated. Why? Because I love my team. I am a Cubs fan in the strongest sense of the term. I refuse to give up hope, no matter how bleak things look.

My wife says that in all relationships, one has to jump in with both feet and commit. Otherwise, it leaves the other side feeling uncertain, empty, and resentful. To truly love someone, you have to be a participant, not just a spectator. When you're a participant, you are invested in the outcome and that means you're vulnerable. That can be a scary place to be. You stand a very real chance of getting hurt in the process. Most of us don't like that feeling, least of all, a bystander.

But you can't live life fully if you're not involved in it.

The Bible, which to me is the best explanation of true love ever written, is filled with verses about God promising to never forsake His children despite all our failings. In other words, He is a fan of ours for life. He believes in us even when we fumble the ball. Or run out-of-bounds. Or hit a foul. Even when we are mathematically eliminated from ever succeeding in the eyes of the world, God will still be there, cheering us on. He'll stay even after all the lights on the field have been turned out and there's no one left in the locker room but us. He is committed. He is a participant in our lives. He sees us as winners. He won't walk out on us before the end of the season, no matter how badly we're performing. And actually, it's when we get to that point of hopelessness that God can finally step in and help us. Like a good coach, He'll inspire us to get back in the game, He'll pump us up to go "show 'em what we're made of," and He'll remind us of our worth to the team. And if we're no longer sabotaging our efforts with our own pride and our own ideas on how to do things, we can't help but win.

I don't know about you, but too often I want to write the script my way. I allow my ego, not God, to continually pump me up with the illusion that I am more than I am. Or I allow my failures to define me. Left to my own resources, I can convince myself that I am either "da man" or a total loser. I am neither. I am just a formerly angry comic who's trying his best to let God change him from the inside out.

Some days I feel like I'm not doing enough with whatever talents God has given me. I am so thankful for the healing God has and continues to give my family and me. But I feel like I'm not doing enough. I feel guilty for not being out there making the touchdowns, the home runs, the goals, and the baskets for the One who believed in me when few others did. It's easy to convince ourselves that only those who are making the big plays in life are the ones He notices—the Billy Grahams, the Mother Teresas, the ones who stand out in our minds as truly making an impact on the world.

But God needs us second-stringers too. He needs the water boys and the batboys and even the cheerleaders. He needs us all to be participants in this game of life because when it comes to us, He's already made a total emotional investment. He gave us everything He had.

As I write this, professional golfer Phil Mickelson has just put on the green jacket of the Masters Tournament. I have been a big fan of Phil's game for years. Whenever he walked down the stretch, I was as nervous as he was. I have followed his career and have felt for him each time the media has thrown the monkey of never winning the "big one" onto his back.

But his game is not why I bring up his name. I bring it up because I've come to realize how much each one of us needs our fans. Those who will stand on the sidelines and cheer us on to bigger and better feats no matter how many times we've dropped the ball. Those who will believe in us when all the others have long since walked away.

God is that kind of fan. When it comes to our lives, He is no bystander. Not only do I believe this truth, I cling to it with all of my heart. This is why it is so important for me to read the Bible. It's not just a book about God's promises; it's also a book of admonitions, praise, and encouragement. It's my own personal affirmation book. It tells me that I am not a loser. It tells me that I have worth. No matter how tough things may seem at any given moment, it tells me that I don't have to run away. It's all written there just for you and me. But be warned, it's powerful. You can't possibly read about how much God believes in you and still feel like a failure. You can't possibly read about His loyalty to your "team" and feel like your family and you are in this life alone. You can't read about His unconditional, fanatical love and not feel compelled to return the same to Him.

I've always felt that life is kind of like a cartoon I used to watch called *Tooter Turtle*. I have talked to a lot of people over the years, and the majority of them don't remember ever having seen this cartoon, so perhaps it was shown only in the Chicago area. Tooter was a turtle who, like most kids, was restless and full of big dreams. Not happy with just being an adolescent turtle and enjoying his turtle toys, he wanted bigger and better things, which also meant bigger responsibilities. So he would go to the Wizard and ask him to give him whatever his heart desired. In one episode, he told the Wizard to turn him into a fireman. The Wizard advised the young lad that being a fireman is a dangerous job, but Tooter didn't want to hear any of this. He just begged the Wizard, who eventually acquiesced.

At first, being a fireman was fun for the little turtle, but as in life, not all things work out the way we've planned. The next thing Tooter knew, he was in the middle of a burning building, screaming for the Wizard to take him back to his regular life where it was safe.

"Help me, Mr. Wizard!" Tooter cried. "I don't want to be a fireman anymore! I just want to be a kid."

Isn't that the way it is with us much of the time? We beg for something, and then when it doesn't work out, we scream for God to come and save us from our own request. In spite of our shortsightedness, things do seem to work out over time, as promised in Romans 8:28. In spite of our running, in spite of our hiding, in spite of our feelings of worthlessness, God still uses us. No one knows this more than I.

I was forty years old when Christ captured my heart. Being that age allowed me to look back over my life and see things that someone younger than I was might not have noticed. The first thing I had to admit was that the most painful places of my life were where the most growth took place. If it hadn't been for the pain, I may not have been pushed to make the changes that were so necessary in my life.

Sometimes life isn't all that funny for a comedian. We're human. We have our ups and downs just like everyone else. We just wear our masks a little more often. But when I came to a point in my life where I was losing everything—my marriage was on the verge of a divorce, we owed everyone, and I was getting through my days taking anything I could get my hands on—I knew I had to do something. And I did. I gave up. I gave up control. I gave up my doubts. I gave up my fears. God healed my marriage, gave me back everything I had lost and more, and I've been sober now for almost twenty years.

The biggest change in my life, though, has been that of going from spectator to participant. It hasn't been easy. This bystander is much more comfortable warming benches. But investing in life and relationships, becoming vulnerable, and involving and trusting God with my everyday affairs have made all the difference in my life.

Another thing that I've learned as a participant is that everyone on the field has a purpose. We can't all be quarterbacks. In fact, some of us will never get the attention that the star players get. But God still uses and needs each one of us, even those who may feel that what they're doing isn't making much of an impact on anyone's life.

Years ago, I was in the car with Ryan, who was about nine or ten at the time. We were chatting away, not talking about anything in particular, when he asked if I had ever accepted Jesus Christ as my Lord and Savior. I was listening this time, and to his surprise I said, "Yes, as a matter of fact I have."

"When?" he asked.

"About a month ago, in August," I said.

"I gave my life to Jesus in June," he said.

"Well, aren't you the seasoned Christian!" I joked.

Ryan smiled but then said, "You know, Daddy, me and Aaron prayed for you and Mommy every Saturday."

I looked at him. Prayed for me? Where? Along with one of those television preachers? Or had he been sneaking out of the house and attending Billy Graham crusades?

None of the above.

You see, there was this lady in our neighborhood who held a little Bible study with some of the neighborhood children every week. When she first approached me to ask if my sons could attend, I said "Sure." My wife and I were not believers at the time, but I didn't care. I just figured it'd be nice to get them out of the house and have a little peace and quiet for an hour or two. Free babysitting, right?

So my sons went every Saturday and enjoyed it. And they learned. And every week they prayed for their mother and father who didn't have a clue about a God who loved them and had a purpose for their lives.

This selfless woman, who had enough love to invite someone else's children into her home for nothing more than to share God's Word with them and pray with them for their families, was my Billy Graham. Today, I've grown to love and respect Billy Graham, but back then, I would've turned the dial and moved on to the next infomercial rather than hear another preacher tell me how God could change my life.

I was living my life my own way and failing miserably, but a quiet, unassuming neighborhood lady praying with my kids week after week is what finally got through to me. Unless she happens to pick up this book, that kind woman has no idea that all those prayers were finally answered. She moved away before I got a chance to thank her. But I'll be eternally grateful to her for not taking the easy, bystander way out; for, instead, being faithful to that seemingly minor thing God had asked her to do.

Participants come in all shapes, sizes, nationalities, and ages. They're just ordinary people, doing whatever they can to tell someone else that God loves them. They have no way of knowing where those seeds might fall. But the seeds that lady planted in two young boys ended up falling on a very angry comic whom God wanted to change into one of life's participants.

As a new participant, I've tried to plant a few seeds of my own. Today, I use my stand-up comedy to do so not only in comedy clubs, but also in outreach shows at churches all around America. I am humbled by the opportunities God has given me to share my story. I also know that I had nothing to do with any of this. It's all about God finally getting through to a stubborn, scared, A. D. D., hypochondriac bystander and telling him, "You're worth My love." It's about a lady and two little kids who prayed for their mommy and daddy. And it's about an amazing, amazing grace.

Now if you don't mind, the Cubs are playing the Reds. So being the faithful fan that I am, I shall bring this to a close so I can go root for my team. Win or lose, I will never give up hope or stop rooting. Just as God never gives up hope or stops rooting for us.

Life is good, is it not?

"Choose life so that you and
your descendants may live."
Deuteronomy 30:19